ADVANCE PRAISE

"With honesty, generosity, precision, and insight, Hollis writes the story of her life—from her girlhood in rural Oregon, where she both broke and followed the rules, to her hard-earned self-acceptance at middle age. *This Particular Happiness* is a gloriously wise book about one woman's unexpected path to becoming."
—Cheryl Strayed, *New York Times* bestselling author of *Wild*

"*This Particular Happiness* claims an important place in the conversation about what it means to be female, especially a female who doesn't follow the script written by a traditional rural family. Written in honest and intimate chapters, this stunning debut memoir is ultimately a love letter to the power of choice."
—Sheila Hamilton, author of *All the Things We Never Knew*

"Examining every feeling of sorrow, jealousy, need, regret and pain, she unspools her story like the counselor that she is; always asking why, always digging deeper. . . . Beautifully done with an open, honest voice, *This Particular Happiness* is a memoir of childlessness, happiness, and wholeness, and how those disparate things can entwine around a full life."
—Dianah Hughley, bookseller, Powell's City of Books

"This book drew me in from the very first scene and gave me what I want in a memoir: the opportunity to see inside a very particular experience as well as to ponder big questions. What blend of family, culture, and personality inform our expectations? What do we seek from love and intimacy? How do we build defenses against trauma? How do we change? Hollis writes with a clarity and rhythm that makes the reading easy going even as she covers difficult and complex territory. The artful interweaving of storylines and time periods reveals a hard-won wisdom."
—Zoe Zolbrod, author of *The Telling*

"Jackie Shannon Hollis's *This Particular Happiness* doesn't keep secrets. It's bare-naked honest. What a relief. Another sparkling moment of honesty, what we need, what we crave, what we try to remember."

—Leanne Grabel, author of *Brontosaurus: Memoir of a Sex Life*

"*This Particular Happiness* examines the particularly female journey—how and where do we make room for love? And whether lover, wife, mother, or daughter, how can we be our most authentic selves? Jackie Shannon Hollis explores this rich terrain with clarity and courage, in spare and lovely prose evocative of the high plains landscape and fertile farmland she hails from."

—Jennie Shortridge, author of *Love Water Memory*

"*This Particular Happiness* is the eloquent unfolding of Jackie Shannon Hollis's lifelong understanding of and relationship to her own body: what it could do for her, how it could be used against her, and, ultimately, how she claimed it as her own. Her prose is both achingly beautiful and precise, underscoring the journey of discovering integrity to oneself, and the promise of true love."

—Liz Prato, author of *Volcanoes, Palm Trees, and Privilege: Essays on Hawaii*

"Sit down. Make tea. Hold *This Particular Happiness* by Jackie Shannon Hollis in your hands and read it slowly because she has written you a love letter. Maybe the intimacy in this prose comes from the tender way she observes. Maybe it's the lyrical prose flexing, revealing the complicated choices one couple makes under the pressures of small towns, big events, changing times, and the relentless pursuit of understanding. Surely, it's her writing that captures her wanting that is as open as the wheat country that formed her. In this love letter, you will find your own 'beautiful ache.'"

—Kate Gray, author of *Carry the Sky*

"Jackie Shannon Hollis takes a topic that is typically whispered about and stares at it unflinchingly: a woman's decision whether or not to have children. She questions the cultural conditioning (told by movies, television, and our families), along with her own biological and emotional responses, that a childless woman is failing to fulfill her destiny. What she excavates during this psychological dig is the truth that what makes any woman's life successful is the woman herself. A powerful book for both genders and any sexual orientation."

—Kate Carroll de Gutes,
author of *The Authenticity Experiment*

"This deeply engaging memoir wrestles with one of the most important questions of all: Why do we want what we want? Jackie Shannon Hollis explores how her own desires have been shaped by a culture that celebrates 'mother' more than any other role for women, and the possibilities that open up when she chooses not to play the role. A vibrant, absorbing, intimate book."

—Leni Zumas, author of *Red Clocks*

"We all know that having a child changes everything, but so, too, does not having one, and in Hollis's brave, moving memoir, she explores the bliss, the yearning, the making peace with a life she and her partner chose (and didn't choose), and how happiness takes on shapes we can never imagine. The perfect book for anyone contemplating motherhood—or not!"

—Caroline Leavitt, *New York Times* bestselling
author of *Pictures of You*

"Jackie mines the depths of who she is and how she wants to be in this complicated world. She doesn't settle for the obvious path, and even though there's some disappointment and heartbreak, she learns how to love and be loved in just the way she wants. This book is a celebration of living life using your own damn map."

—Yuvi Zalkow, author of *A Brilliant Novel in the Works*

THIS PARTICULAR HAPPINESS

JACKIE SHANNON HOLLIS

FOREST AVENUE PRESS
Portland, Oregon

THIS PARTICULAR HAPPINESS

A Childless Love Story

Content warning: The author wants you know that this is a story of her life, including joys and sadnesses, falling in love, and experiencing the death of loved ones. A sexual assault is also a part of this story. She hopes you will find many beautiful things here, as the painful parts of life can be transformed by sharing our experiences.

Disclaimer: The author has done her best, through memory and conversations with others, to relate the events told in this memoir as factually as possible. In scenes of her husband's childhood, she filled in images from stories he told her. In a few instances, names, identifying characteristics, or specific details of events have been changed to protect the privacy of others without altering the facts relevant to this story.

Library of Congress Cataloging-in-Publication Data

Names: Hollis, Jackie Shannon, 1958- author.
Title: This particular happiness : a childless love story / Jackie Shannon Hollis.
Description: Portland, Oregon : Forest Avenue Press, [2019] | Includes bibliographical references.
Identifiers: LCCN 2019007726 | ISBN 9781942436393 (pbk.)
Subjects: LCSH: Hollis, Jackie Shannon, 1958- | Childfree choice--United States. | Childlessness--United States.
Classification: LCC HQ762.U6 .H65 2019 | DDC 306.87--dc23
LC record available at https://lccn.loc.gov/2019007726

Mrs. Stevens Hears the Mermaids Singing by May Sarton (copyright © May Sarton) reproduced by permission of W.W. Norton and Company.

Thanks to *The Sun* magazine, *Rosebud*, *Mary Journal*, *VoiceCatcher*, and *Flashquake*, where some of the material in *This Particular Happiness* first appeared.

1 2 3 4 5 6 7 8 9

Distributed by Publishers Group West

Printed in the United States of America

Forest Avenue Press LLC
P.O. Box 80134
Portland, OR 97280
forestavenuepress.com

In memory of Mom.
Thank you for always watching over me.

And to Bill.
Thank you for holding up the mirror,
even when it is heavy.

"Love opens the doors into everything, as far as I can see, including and perhaps most of all, the door into one's own secret, and often terrible and frightening, real self."

—May Sarton, *Mrs. Stevens Hears the Mermaids Singing*

FOREWORD
By Jody Day

BECAUSE OF MY WORK supporting involuntarily childless women, I am a vault of private stories, and I often long for those stories to be out in the world so that others might find them and feel less alone. Thus, I finished reading *This Particular Happiness: A Childless Love Story* with a feeling of great satisfaction, as Jackie Shannon Hollis has done a superb job of articulating one of the many threads woven into the tapestry of modern childlessness—that of being "childless by relationship."

So many women come to me in the throes of making the very same decision that Jackie had to make—of choosing between the love of a partner and the chance to become a mother—and their main fear is often, "But what if I end up resenting him so much it destroys us?" This memoir works through how Jackie's husband's choice not to become a father played out in their marriage and lives over many years, and it does so in a way that feels utterly authentic to me—with her at times pleading for him to change his mind, and at other moments grateful for the opportunities they have as a childless couple to give their love to the many children in their lives while still having the time to explore their passions for travel and, in Jackie's case, writing.

Reading this book immediately after Sheila Heti's *Motherhood*, I felt that I'd experienced both sides of the coin of maternal and nonmaternal longing, and the incredibly complex issues that have to be unpacked by modern women to make peace with voluntary or involuntary childlessness. Those who have not walked these paths often imagine that women without children either "didn't want them" or "couldn't have them," but the truth is far, far more complex.

This book also took me deep into the daily experience of growing up to become the only childless woman in a large, rural, traditional American family, and the very texture of that life lingers on in me as if I'd been watching a film of wide-open spaces, waving corn, and close-knit families. People often imagine that the hardest part of childlessness is not having a baby, but in fact it's a lifelong social and emotional loss that resonates across every aspect of our lives. This book is wonderful at both illuminating that loss and illustrating ways to deal with it. It also addresses the understandable envy some parents feel about the freedom and possibilities inherent in childlessness, and gives a picture of the emotional costs they might be unaware of. This book shows both sides, and does so with courageous honesty and great tenderness toward all involved.

I recommend this book with great pleasure to any childless woman on the path of self-healing and to the men, mothers, and others in our lives who want to understand what it takes to make peace with not doing the "one thing" that society still expects of every woman, whether she can, will, or wants to be a mother.

Jody Day is the author of *Living the Life Unexpected: 12 Weeks to Your Plan B for a Meaningful and Fulfilling Future Without Children* and the founder of www.gateway-women.com.

I.
THE SHOUT OF
MOTHERHOOD

1. THE WOMAN THINGS

THE CHILD IN MY arms breathed the fast breath of baby sleep. Her eyes moved beneath her lids and her mouth pouted and relaxed, pouted and relaxed. I smoothed my hand over her thick black hair, smelled the smell of her, milk and powder and Desitin. Her small weight and the heat of her against my chest were perfect comforts that stilled me.

It was 1990. I was thirty-one years old and a month into my second marriage on that weekend in May. My husband, Bill, and I had made the three-hour drive from our home in Portland, Oregon, to the family ranch just outside my hometown of Condon.

My sisters and sister-in-law and I were gathered at the round oak table in the kitchen nook. Mom was at the counter chopping vegetables for a layered salad. The steady beat of the blade made time against the whine of race cars on the TV in the family room. Bill and Dad and my brothers and brothers-in-law were in there, talking now and then, watching those cars go around.

The roast in the oven filled the kitchen with a familiar smell of home and of a history that went all the way back to my great-grandparents, who settled this wheat and cattle ranch in the north central part of the state. They built this house and raised eight kids in it. The house was passed on to my grandfather and then to my father, who raised his five kids here. My parents still lived in the house, and this was the gathering place whenever I came from Portland for a visit.

My nieces and nephew ran through the kitchen. They were streaks of giggles, blond hair, brown hair, brown hair, blond hair, hard-playing pinked cheeks. On into the family room to ask Dad could they go into the granary? Feed the chickens? Comb Jader, the collie?

I was sunk deep in holding-a-baby love. Alyson was the first child of my younger sister. I'd held her only once before, at my wedding, when she was a month old. My women friends had gathered around us, me the bride, Alyson the newest baby in my world.

I smiled now at Cris. "You did good," I said.

My older sister, Leanne, watched. I figured she was thinking this baby would get a good dose of the love I gave to her two girls and to my brother's two kids as well. She nodded toward the baby.

"Holding her," she said, "does it make you want to have one?"

A sharp catch in my chest, the small arrow of hope in Leanne's question.

Mom stopped chopping and turned for my answer.

Leanne had a careful smile, like maybe she shouldn't have asked but couldn't stop herself, this moment so right, me so clearly adoring this baby.

"Oh, I don't know," I said, trying to think of how to say it. That yes, holding Alyson did make me want to have one. But no, I wasn't going to.

Most of my life I thought I'd end up being a mother. But things had changed. I'd changed in a way that drew me toward a life different from what I'd been raised for.

Somewhere along the line I'd told Leanne, told Mom, too, that Bill and I didn't plan to have kids. Up until this moment

I'd been settled with this. No one had tried to talk me out of it. We weren't the kind of family to question each other's decisions, or mostly we weren't. There were exceptions. This seemed to be one.

Mom set the knife down and moved closer. She looked at the baby. At me with the baby. "It's our only disappointment," she said, "about you marrying Bill." From the pressure of her words like a held-back horse coming out of the gate, from the angle of her jaw, the way she leaned in, she'd been holding this thought for a while. "You're missing out on the biggest joy in life," she said.

I looked at the baby. My scalp prickled. All eyes on me, the only woman in the room who didn't have kids. The room was quiet except for the racing cars. Except for the beat of my heart. The breath of the baby.

This felt like an intervention. It felt like an argument I couldn't win.

Bill must've heard all this over the whine of those cars. He called out from the family room. "Aren't *I* Jackie's biggest joy?" The tease in it, a call to me that covered his worry.

"It's not the same," Mom said, quick and harsh. "Having a child is like no love you've ever felt."

Bill went quiet. I wanted to go to him. To stand in the doorway and protect him from her sure jab.

From the family room, Dad said, "It's not our business, Jeanie." The calm and patience of his voice didn't hide his silent command: *Stop.*

My sisters were quiet. The men in the other room were quiet. Dad speaking up to Mom like this surprised me.

A few years earlier, not long after my first marriage had ended, Dad told me he hoped each of us kids would have five kids, just like he did. "That'd be twenty-five grandkids," he'd said.

"Twenty-five." I'd laughed at the accuracy of his math. The extravagance of his hope. I brushed past it, with a joke about how the others had better get to work making babies because he shouldn't count on me.

The conversations Dad and Mom must've had. The two of them, maybe in the family room, her with a crossword, him with the TV. Mom saying, "Jackie said she and Bill aren't having kids." Dad saying he'd figured that out. Or in bed at night, them next to each other in the dark. Her saying she was disappointed. Him saying he'd hoped for more grandkids.

Their disappointment moved into me. I opened my mouth to speak, like I might find a right answer.

Mom said, "I'm just worried." She softened her voice a little. "Worried you'll end up being a bitter, lonely old woman. Like your Aunt Lena."

Alyson still slept in my arms. My shirt was damp from the heat she put off.

I didn't know what Mom meant. My great aunt Lena wasn't bitter. All her life, up until she died, she had a smile every time I saw her.

I tried to keep my voice this-is-no-big-deal calm. "I won't," I said. My throat felt tight. I put my head down and pretended all my attention was on this baby.

Mom went back to the counter, knife in hand. She started chopping in quick beats.

I breathed, tried to gather myself, the splintery feeling of knowing I was a disappointment. My sisters moved on to some other topic. Minutes went by. Minutes where I thought I could stop the tears coming up in me. Then knowing I couldn't. I gave the baby back to Cris. Smiled a fake smile. Didn't look anyone in the eye.

I went into the bathroom and sat on the edge of the claw-foot tub. Took a long breath. Tried to get that breath past the clench in my throat. The brass pulls of the dresser next to the sink had dulled over the years. The first two drawers still held ribbons and hairbrushes and pink foam rollers, old lipsticks and broken necklaces and dull tweezers from when my sisters and I lived here. The third drawer down had Mom's secret things that I used to look at before I knew what they were. I'd kept looking after Mom explained the woman things to me, when I was still waiting to be old enough to use them myself. Pads and tampons and sprays and creams.

I'd been the second-to-last one in my class to start bleeding. I'd felt left behind. Sometimes I snuck one of those pads and wore it to pretend.

The murmur of the women in the kitchen came through the walls. The kids called out to one another. Their bright voices. I wanted to slide to the floor. Tears pushed against my throat, mouth, eyes. I must not cry. It would show on me. Mom would feel bad that she'd said anything. Everyone would know her words shoved open a door I thought I'd closed.

The scent of soap and musty towels and the cinnamon perfume of potpourri came to me in a long breath. I stood up. In the mirror over the sink, my dark eyes had the pinched-in look of held back tears. "It's okay," I said. Another breath, hard to take in. "It's okay," I said again.

2. WE PRACTICED. WE PRETENDED.

DURING MY CHILDHOOD IN the 1960s almost all the women in our small town were mothers. They had two, three, five, eight children. By the time Mom was twenty-four, she had four kids. Pat, Brad, Leanne, and me, the youngest.

The mothers of Condon drove big boaty cars or station wagons with kids piled all the way into the back. Some of the women worked. Mom worked when money was tight. She started her first job as an assistant to the local doctor when I was six years old. Even though she wasn't a nurse, she wore a white dress and white shoes with rubber soles that sounded like whispers when she walked. Her job seemed like that too, a whisper compared to the shout of motherhood.

More important than helping their husbands on the land or working in the offices and stores was that these women were our mothers. They cooked and baked, cleaned and washed, knitted and sewed. They watched us go off to backyards or barns or canyons to play, dropped us off at the swimming pool every day of summer; they called us in to eat, checked homework and dirty hands, bathed us and cut our hair, read to us and sang to us. They took turns bringing cookies and decorations to school holiday parties, threw birthday parties, organized Cub Scouts and 4-H and Brownies. They gathered to drink coffee and teach each other crafts: crochet and knitting, sewing and macramé and upholstery. They taught these things to their daughters. How to do everything.

They were pretty and smart and strong. My mom most of all. When she brought the treats to school parties, she dressed in the latest. Slim and lipsticked, her dark hair showed off high cheekbones and the angled lines of her jaw. She brought Valentine cupcakes with frosting hearts, Christmas tree cookies with silver beads for ornaments. I made sure everyone knew she was my mom. I wanted to be like her. And above all, the one thing I never questioned was that I would be a mother too.

MY SISTER AND FRIENDS and I played house with our baby dolls more than we played nurse or school or Go Fish. My doll had eyes that blinked. Her soft belly and bottom had a heft like a real baby. When I turned her over, she let out a sad cry. I wrapped my baby in the triangle of a blanket and fed her. The white liquid in the bottle flowed like real milk. I held my baby up to burp her, her head next to mine, light pats on her back, whispers in her ear. Anyone watching would think she was a real baby, that I was a real mother.

MOM AND DAD GATHERED us kids together in the family room one evening when I was seven. We sat in a row on the sofa, Dad in an easy chair in front of us. Mom turned the TV off and perched next to Dad on the arm of the chair. Their serious faces turned into let's-all-be-excited faces, with big eyes and big smiles. They said we were going to have a little sister or brother soon.

I took on a fast, hard pout: lower lip stuck out, head hung down.

"Why?" I said.

I shared left-handedness with Dad and my brother Brad, being a girl with my sister Leanne, brown hair and brown eyes with Mom. I shared my parents' names. They were Jack and Jeanie. I was Jacklyn Jean. Everything about me was shared. Being the baby of the family was my one special thing.

I pouted all through Mom's pregnancy. Mom said, "Can't you be nice? Be happy for someone else." Being nice was a big thing in our family. But I felt weak against myself. Dad said, "If that lower lip sticks out any farther, a bird's going to come along and poop on it."

My pouting didn't stop my little sister Cris from being born on the day before I turned eight. Mom missed my birthday. Everyone said Cris was my present. I didn't get a special cake like Mom always made for birthdays. I pouted some more.

Everyone said the baby had brown eyes even bigger than mine. Everyone said she was beautiful. Mom showed me how to cradle the baby's head when I held her, how to heat a bottle and test it with drips of formula on my wrist. She taught me about burping and soft spots and diaper rash and how to put a wet diaper directly in the diaper bin and how to dip a poopy one in the toilet first.

My pouting got boring even for me. I started to like this baby. I still had bouts of jealousy and even teased Cris, and maybe I tripped her when she was learning to walk. Once I gave her a peppercorn to bite, which made her cry and made Mom mad enough to put Tabasco sauce on my tongue.

But mostly I felt glad for my little sister. She needed love and help. The urine ammonia smell, the poop smell, the sour spit-up became part of the love I felt for her, equal alongside baby powder and gentle shampoo and her giggle when I played and acted silly for her. She trusted me when she slept in my arms.

When we were out in the world, I carried her like Mom did, with one hip jutted out, one arm holding her, like I'd been doing this forever.

This is what I did. This is what my girlfriends did. With dolls, with little sisters and brothers, with the children we babysat. We pretended. We practiced. We prepared. Our mothers said to us, "When you grow up." "When you have your own children." No question. We would grow up. We would have children of our own.

3.GOOD HOUSEKEEPING

THROUGH THE REST OF the afternoon and into the evening on that visit home with Bill, I acted like what Mom had said while I held Alyson was a conversation like any other, even though I was sure the impact of her words showed on me like a blue-and-purple bruise. Inside me a thick chunk of hurt lodged high in my belly. I helped set up for dinner and avoided eye contact with everyone. I laughed extra loud with my nieces and nephew.

Bill sat next to me while we ate. He held my hand; he put his arm around me. I could hardly stand his touch. I felt myself taking a hard turn from the three good years we'd had together, from the falling in love and the love that came after the falling. Just a month before, I had stood up in front of friends and family and said yes, I would be with him forever, yes, I would go through anything with him. Saying yes meant being fine with not having kids. I didn't want him to see the question that had started in me. Maybe marrying him had been a mistake.

Another part of me wanted to fight. It was nineteen-god-damn-ninety. Modern times. I wasn't Mom or of her genera-tion, where having kids was all a woman could do. Women had choices. I didn't have to have kids to know joy. I had a career. A job I loved and was proud of. My counseling degree had led me to my current position as clinical supervisor. I had thought Mom was proud of this too.

I ticked off a mental list of all the ways Mom was wrong. Maybe early on, when we were first born, she felt that joy. But had she forgotten all that came after? The hurricane of a mess that five kids bring. The way she used to yell at us, threaten us with the rubber spatula and sometimes use it. Did she forget how kids scream and cry and get sick one after the other so that she was always wiping up puke or shit or snot? The way we could lie and hide and sneak? Didn't she remember how we mocked her when we got old enough to fall out of love with her, mocked the way she laughed, the way she cleared her throat, the way she sat with her legs crossed and tucked. Our sullen eye-rolls at anything she might suggest we do. Didn't she remember the fights between us kids that turned to fights with her? The ways she fell apart. Precious things in shards, broken bones, stitches and scars, car wrecks and drunken arrivals home. That didn't look like joy, not one bit.

LATE IN THE EVENING my brothers and sisters left, taking the kids with them, Leanne's girls still asking couldn't they stay the night. I didn't push for them to stay like I usually did.

Then it was Mom and Dad and Bill and me. The TV was on. Some cop show. Dad nodded off in his recliner, and Mom went back and forth from the family room to the last bits of clean-up in the kitchen.

Bill and I watched that cop show. I yawned and said I was tired. A way to distract Bill from my quiet. Inside me that chunk of hurt kept turning, pushing up against my love for him.

Pretty soon Dad went to bed. The cop show ended, and Bill headed to bed too. I told him I'd be up soon. I didn't want to be alone with him, not yet. I felt scared by this turning in me, and I didn't want it to scare him.

Now Mom and I were alone. An old movie came on. I picked up a *Good Housekeeping* magazine. Mom sat in her chair and looked back and forth from the TV to a how-to book on stained glass.

I wanted to tell her how much I loved Bill. She couldn't have missed how many boys and men I'd gone through to find him. He was the one I'd chosen. We had joy, just the two of us.

She must have forgotten how good just two could be. She and Dad were only married for a year before they had Pat. Then the next three kids came along, one after the other. The stress of us, plus her ulcers and migraines, and the years when dad drank must have blocked out the memory of that one year when it was just the two of them.

I wished Mom would look at me. That she would see I was hurting. Take back what she'd said. Maybe it wasn't too late to stop this thing from growing in me. The wanting to please her, to please Dad, to be what was expected.

I paged through recipes and good-housekeeping things. I could've asked her what she meant about Aunt Lena being a bitter, lonely old woman. My great aunt Lena had been in her eighties when she'd died a few years earlier, so I couldn't argue with the old part. She'd married late and, like me, had been ten years younger than her husband, who'd died when Aunt Lena was in her forties. They'd had no kids.

She was part of our family, always there for Easter and Christmas and any other big-dinner holiday at our house or at our grandparents' house, giving each of us an envelope with a ten-dollar bill. She seemed busy and smart, with friends to see and clubs to go to and a pretty little house full of special things. She made us laugh; she made us feel loved. We were safe with her. Bitter was the last word I'd have put to her.

But Nana, our grandmother, got our priority. She had first choice on babysitting and special times. We were with her most Saturday nights and for Sunday dinners and after school when Mom had meetings. Aunt Lena's invitations for us to come to her house hardly ever got taken up. Maybe she'd wanted more of us than she got. Maybe she had been lonely. Maybe Mom had seen a bitterness when she took care of Aunt Lena in her dying year. Maybe they'd talked of the absence of a child.

Mom's head was tilted down to her book, the light of the lamp behind her, the flicker of the TV in front of her. That old movie, women in dresses, men in suits.

I held on to what was in me, the possible things I could say, the questions I could ask. Finally, I stood up. "Well, I guess I'll go to bed."

Mom looked up and smiled. "Good night, hon. I hope you sleep well."

We weren't the kind of mother and daughter who went back and sorted things out.

"See you in the morning," I said to the room, to the lamplight, to her in her chair.

4. FLICKER SHADOWS

THROUGH MY GROWING-UP YEARS, the flicker shadows from the TV were a constant in our family room. We turned it on when we woke in the mornings, and Mom kept it on until well after we went to bed at night. The TV music and chatter and laughter and tears became the backdrop that took the place of other conversations we might have had.

On school nights, Mom sat on the sofa, and I sat on the linoleum floor in front of her, and we watched TV while she put curlers in my hair. I admired the long legs and synchronized moves of the June Taylor Dancers. I never missed a Miss America pageant. I watched Mary Tyler Moore be the wife of Dick Van Dyke and Lucille Ball be the wife of Desi Arnaz in reruns of *I Love Lucy*. These housewives spent their days doing funny things they had to hide from their husbands. They slept in twin beds. They had kids who were cute and mostly perfect, and being a mom looked perfect too.

Each week, Eva Gabor cried out her longing for Park Avenue on *Green Acres*, and Mom bopped me on the head with the tooth end of the rat-tail comb if I laughed too much and caused her to lose strands of my hair from her hold. The *Green Acres* wife didn't have kids, and she seemed silly and vain, but she stayed loyal to her husband, who wanted to be a farmer.

Some women on TV didn't have kids. On *The Andy Griffith Show* old Aunt Bee worried endlessly about her nephew Andy and his son Opie. Sometimes she got flustered, but she always had the best advice, the most comfort. Miss Kitty on *Gunsmoke* was strong and wise and a business owner who'd saved up her bartending wages and bought the Long Branch Saloon. Plus she loved the sheriff.

The hairstyles Mom created for me in front of the TV went from ringlets to loose curls to the shortest Twiggy cut. She stopped doing my hair in my middle-school years when I decided to grow it out long and straight. Then I spent time in front of the TV brushing my own hair and practicing braids.

The TV women changed like my hairstyles. Mary Tyler Moore got her own show. She went from being Dick Van Dyke's anxious wife to a single woman, working in news. Lucille Ball went from being Desi's wife to being a widow with kids who were so rarely on screen that it seemed like she didn't have kids at all. Mostly she was Mr. Mooney's secretary.

Carol Burnett had her own show and the men were funny sidekicks.

Sandy Duncan and Rhoda and Charlie's Angels were headliners. These women lived another kind of life, a life of career and city. Even though they dated and longed for a man, even though their bosses were always men, these women didn't have kids, and that looked like a fine life too.

Real-life men on TV did big things I thought I'd like to do too. *The Undersea World of Jacques Cousteau* came on every Sunday night. I imagined myself in the gray ocean, brave against sharks and manta rays. I followed Mike Wallace and Harry Reasoner asking *60 Minutes* of serious questions with concerned looks on their faces. On Saturday and Sunday afternoons, men boxed and raced and skied. I could be Mario Andretti, Jackie Stewart, Jean-Claude Killy. I could be brave. I could speak clear, sure words, ask questions, be smart, go fast.

5. THIS UNLOOSED THING

THAT NIGHT, AFTER I left Mom with the TV and her how-to book on stained glass, I went up to my old bedroom. A dull light came up from the gridded vent in the floor that opened from the living room below. I undressed by this light.

I got into the old bed, knowing its wiry voice, how to keep it from telling every move. I stretched out on my back, not close to Bill like usual. I didn't turn to kiss him good night. He put a hand on my thigh in a slow, sleepy way. Tears started, slipping down from the corners of my eyes.

Bill leaned up on one elbow. "What's wrong?" He put a hand on my shoulder, ready to listen like he always listened when I shared my hurting with him.

"What Mom said. About us not having kids." The crying moved up from my belly and chest, in whispery sobs. Trying to be quiet. To not let Mom hear. Old house. Sounds carry.

Bill pulled me to him. He held me. Touched my hair, my back, my shoulders, my arms. He said, "Oh, honey." So soft. So tender. He held me until my breath found its pace again.

Enough space in that breath for me to say, "I want to have a baby." Abrupt. Sudden. It made no sense.

My words hovered in the dark, small clouds of white air in a cool room.

Bill loosened his hands. He rolled onto his back. "We talked about this, Jackie." A surprise in his voice. The unexpected.

"I know." We had talked about it. No children. I'd agreed. Willingly. Happily. Lovingly.

"I thought you were okay with it," he said.

We'd made plans for our future. Bill was just past forty and would retire at fifty from his job as a firefighter. I'd work ten more years after that. We'd be free to travel and play and be together, just the two of us. But not just the two of us, because our life and travel and play often included friends and family. Now, those plans looked pale and washed out next to the idea of a child in my arms.

"I *was* okay with it." A longing surged in me as if it had been waiting for just this moment. "I'm not anymore."

I wanted to sit with my sisters and hold my own baby in the nook of the kitchen. I turned toward him. "I want to have a baby."

I hardly breathed. Maybe in my quiet and stillness, he would see how much I wanted this. It would be that easy.

"I'm clear, Jackie." He used my name when he was most serious. His voice was calm, patient. "I don't want kids," he said.

I'd heard this kind of calm before from Bill. He didn't argue or justify when he knew what he wanted and didn't want, what he would do and wouldn't do. I'd loved and respected this about him. But now I resented his sureness and the quiet way he said it.

He reached for me, and I cried again. "Okay," I said, "okay. I know." My voice sounded weak.

He held me. I let him. This man refusing me what I wanted, comforted me in the pain of not having it. I wanted to hate him. But he had to be as stunned as I. My whiplash change from no to yes was a betrayal.

We stayed there, his arms around me. Me still and silent.

His breath lengthened. In his sleep, his hold lightened.

The murmur of the TV downstairs came up through the vent. Mom down there with her movie, her book, her worries for me. Bill was sleeping. The hurt from Mom seeped into anger. His refusal had been so certain. So final. I moved as far away in the bed as I could. Held myself at the edge, even though the old mattress wanted to tip us together.

The wanting unloosed in me had already grown too big to shove back down. The only thing that could make it go away chanted inside me: *A baby, a baby, a baby.*

6. THE KNOWING WAS IN ME

BIRTH AND MOTHERING, SEPARATION and death were right out our picture window, on every walk to the barn or canyon, and in the meat on our nightly dinner table. In addition to what I learned from my mother and the mothers of Condon, I took in the lessons of the ranch.

Every year in midwinter, our herd of black cattle stood out against snow or frost or freezing fog. I knew what it meant when one cow was off by herself, back arched, tail raised. A calf on the way. I knew the slippery release that would follow after a time of hunching and hoof-stomping. The calf would fall to the ground, still wet and matted with blood and the birth sac that its mother would lick away with her rough tongue.

This knowing was in me from before I could remember learning it.

The cows nursed. The calves grew. Sometimes one cow would have a handful of calves around her while the others wandered and grazed. They seemed to hand off babysitting duty one to another, to give each other a break. But before the herd moved, mothers and calves found each other again through some call or scent or a bond that no one else could see.

•

FOR A FEW WINTERS in a row Dad bought a handful of bummer lambs from a sheep rancher. Bummers were lambs that had been rejected by a ewe, or she'd had twins and she only allowed one to nurse, or the mother had died.

I was small: six, seven, eight. I helped Dad fill the glass bottles with water and powdered milk, topped them with long black nipples. Dad shook the bottles, and the foamy bubbles gave off a smell of licorice and dust.

We bundled up and went to the barn. Our breath made small clouds that led the way. Our shoes crunched frozen ground. Dad slid the barn door open and we went to the inner stall where the lambs gathered in the light of a single bulb. The nut scent of hay and the smell of horse and leather settled in my throat.

The lambs crowded around us, eager for the milk. I took off my gloves and touched them. Their coiled new wool felt like a million tiny circles. Lambs were my favorite baby animals of all.

Dad held a bottle in each hand but I could only manage one. The warm glass warmed my fingers. A lamb put its mouth on the long black nipple and drank. It bent its front legs low to tilt the bottle down, pushing, pushing. I sturdied my knees and planted my feet and held myself steady for that lamb. The bottle and I were as close to a mother as the lamb would get.

The milk was gone fast. The lambs stayed close when we moved to leave the barn.

On the way back to the house, Dad held my hand in his gloved hand. The leather was thick and warm against my thin knit gloves.

"Couldn't we bring them to the house?" One freezing night the winter before, we'd had a newborn calf in a big cardboard box in the family room.

"No, babe," Dad said. "They'll be fine." The empty bottles rattled in the crate he carried on his other side.

•

CATS SUNNED ON OUR back porch and jumped on blowing grass in the front yard. They brought mice from the barn and toyed them slowly to death. They came running when Dad poured milk fresh from the cows into the pan by the back steps.

Over the course of spring and summer, I watched to see who was pregnant. When they slimmed down from birth and packed full milky nipples, I followed them.

One mother led me to her kittens nested in a manger. They curled around each other in a circle of hay softened by the mother's fur. Their eyes weren't yet open. I picked up each one and welcomed it with the touch of my hand and pressed my cheek against its milk-rounded belly.

One day I returned to the nest and found them a bloody mess. I felt sick in my stomach and scared. They were gone but still there. Pieces and parts. I ran to the house and brought Dad back to look.

His answer: "Well, babe, that happens sometimes. It might have been a tomcat. They don't like to share."

Now I watched the males on our land and tracked their difference. Toms wouldn't share; bulls mounted but did nothing more when it came to birth and raising the young.

7. A PLACE TO SLIP THROUGH

BILL HAD TOLD ME that when he was a boy, becoming a father wasn't something he dreamed of or planned for. This didn't change as he got older.

Now I sorted the stories he'd told me, things I'd seen. I searched for reasons and clues, a door ajar, a place to slip through.

Maybe to change his mind.

Maybe to change my mind.

A FEW SUMMERS AFTER we met, Bill and I went on a beach vacation with his family. One afternoon, I was downstairs playing cards with Bill's sister and brother and Mom. Bill was upstairs being wild-fun uncle with his nieces and nephews like I was silly-fun aunt with mine. The difference with Bill was that he enjoyed the kids when they could talk and tease and play. He never showed an interest in babies.

Shouts and jumping and kid laughs broke through the serious business of dealing cards and making bids. Bill yelled, "Leaping Lizards!" A thump and thud followed by kid screams and shouts.

I looked up at the ceiling, for the plaster that might fall on us. "The kids sure are having fun up there."

"Uh-huh," Bill's mother said with a loving eye roll. "Especially the biggest one." The curve of her mouth held love for her son.

She was eighteen when she had Bill. He was her second child. By the time her third baby came a year and a half later, her husband, their father, had left. Left her. Left them. Bill didn't know the reason. It was possible his dad was overwhelmed by all those kids. A man who didn't like to share his wife, his time, the quiet.

Bill's mom had told me that Bill raised her as much as she raised him. She was almost sixty, but she still needed him. Bill and his brother took her wherever she needed to go because she didn't drive, and they helped out when money was tight for her and Bill's stepfather.

His mother had never asked us if we were going to have kids, even though it was clear we were making a life together.

Maybe she didn't think it was her business.

Maybe she was fine with not having to share.

Maybe she was the kind of mom who didn't place her worries and disappointments on her child.

8. A PLACE FOR A GIRL

My brother Pat raised a pig for 4-H. He named her Petunia. Within a year she went from pink little piglet to grown-up sow with a bunch of pink piglets of her own.

I wanted to raise a pig too. I wanted to show a pig at the fair. Dad said, "That's not for girls."

He liked me to be outside with him. Why wouldn't he want me to have a pig?

I knew better than to look to Mom for help or explanation. In third grade, I'd come home from school full of the news that I'd beaten a boy at arm wrestling. I ran off the bus, through the gate, up the sidewalk and the three steps to our porch. I couldn't wait to tell her. I thought she'd be proud too. She always pointed out my strong shoulders and arms.

She was in the kitchen and I burst out my news. Her eyes went big. She moved in toward me, already shaking her head. "Oh no," she said. Her voice was fierce. "That's not ladylike. Girls are supposed to let the boys win. Make them feel strong. Otherwise they won't like you."

I'd always felt close to her when she taught us things about being a lady, how to sit with our ankles crossed and our hands folded in our laps, how to say please and thank you and always offer to help with the dishes when we were guests, how to squat, not bend, when wearing a dress. But this didn't make any sense. To pretend would be a lie. Wasn't being strong part of being a lady too?

DAD DIDN'T GIVE US girls any lessons about livestock. What little I knew came from listening and watching. Even then, much of it remained a mystery to me. What kind of cows we had or when to breed or vaccinate, the feed to give an animal, types of wheat and planting cycles, horses and bits and bridles, these were lessons Dad gave to my brothers. They had outside chores meant for boys and men.

We girls were taught to do the inside chores: dishes and laundry, toilets and floors, dinners and vacuuming. The women things. We girls could also ride horses whenever we wanted. We watched the annual cattle brandings, collected eggs, fed scraps to the chickens. Anything outside was our choice—as long as we didn't get in the way.

ONE COLD SPRING A mare got into trouble giving birth. The colt was breech. Dad called Granddad, and he came out with a man who knew horses. They all went to the barn, my brothers too. I bundled up and followed them.

The colt wouldn't come any farther out of the mare than one hoof and a stick leg. The man from town had his arm up inside her all the way to his shoulder, trying to turn the colt. The mare's eyes were wide. Her chest rose and fell as her nostrils flared. Other than that, she was still. I wanted to go to her and put my hand on her muzzle, to stroke her neck. To whisper, "It's okay, It's okay."

Granddad must've caught whatever movement I'd made. "She shouldn't be here," he said. Cold and hard. "Not a place for a girl."

Dad looked at me. I already had my mouth open with reasons I should be allowed. "She can be here," Dad said.

Granddad shook his head and the men went back to work on the horse. I stayed on that top rail with a new kind of love for Dad, him speaking up for me against his own father. Raising pigs and planting wheat weren't jobs for a girl. But where birth and death were, I could be witness.

9. LEAVING DOESN'T MEAN IT'S GONE FROM YOU

BILL AND I PACKED up to head back to Portland in the morning. Leanne and the girls came out to say goodbye. My brother Brad did too.

I was a mess of puffy eyes and the hangover of tears.

Mom hugged me. "You look tired," she said.

"Maybe it's allergies or something," I said. She didn't question that.

Mom and Dad stood on the porch. Bill drove. I rolled down my window. I didn't hide my tears. They all waved, and I waved back until I couldn't see them anymore.

I'd left in tears plenty of times before. I missed home the most at the end of a visit, knowing my whole family lived close to each other, me the one always leaving. Once, when Mom saw I was having a hard time with one of these goodbyes, she hugged me to her. "You know, we all only get together when you're here," she said. "The rest of the time we don't see each other like this. You're the one that brings us together."

Now, Bill drove us down the gravel road, over the cattle guard, past the field with new wheat coming on green and tender. Both of us were quiet, and I wiped at the tears and let out a long slow breath.

Within a few minutes Bill turned onto the highway that led to Condon, a mile north of the ranch.

In town, Main Street was Sunday quiet. We drove past the Liberty Theatre with the dark ticket booth, the flag at the Elks Lodge, the grain elevator to the north with the unlit Christmas star that stays there all year and glows with pale lights only in December. Everything was familiar. Everything made me sad.

CONDON IS A SMALL town in the north part of central Oregon. The climate and soil in the area are good enough for dryland wheat ranches and beef cattle. This is what drew my ancestors.

My great-grandparents left Kansas for the west three days after they married. This was in the late 1800s. They came to the Condon area, bought the property south of town, and built the house I grew up in. They had eight children, including my grandfather and my great Aunt Lena.

My grandfather would eventually marry my grandmother, my Nana, whose family came to the Condon area when she was twelve, traveling from Scotland.

All around the county men and women built their homes; they had children; they worked the soil. In town, stores were built to support those farmers and ranchers. Families grew. Children worked in the stores and on the farms and ranches. Sons married; their wives gave them children. Businesses were passed from parent to child. Land was passed from father to son. The ranch I grew up on passed from my great-grandfather to my grandfather to my father.

The town never grew much over a population of a thousand. Those who didn't take over a farm or a business from their parents or marry someone who did, those who couldn't find other work or who simply wanted to see another part of the world, left. Even so, for those of us who grew up in Condon, the ties to the town and the land and to family are strong. Leaving doesn't mean you're gone from it. Leaving doesn't mean it's gone from you.

A FEW MILES OUT of town, Bill put his hand on my leg. "How are you doing?"

"Not good." Out the window, the landscape streamed by. This place of wide-open skies, low hills covered in the fresh green of spring. At the mountain identifier, Mount Adams stood to the north, Mount Hood to the west.

Bill drove down into the canyon and across the John Day River. I'd taken this road hundreds of times. I knew these twisty curves. We came up out of the canyon, through Wasco, and onto I-84 along the Columbia River.

I wanted Bill to say okay. To say that in the night his mind had changed as much as mine had. I wanted him to say yes. That he'd never considered it before but, *Yes, a child would be just the thing for us.* But he didn't say it.

The Columbia River runs east to west. The highway runs alongside the water. The water is always different depending on weather and wind; it is blue or gray or even green, glass-smooth to rough and white-capped. Today there were small waves, and the water was choppy.

"I'm tired," I said. "I didn't sleep much." I put my seat down and stretched out. In the sky, the clouds were pure white and puffed full, like they were there for fun. I closed my eyes against them. Tears came and went, slipping down the sides of my face. The pull of Mom's disappointment was like a thick cord, behind us, tethering me, pulling me back home to family and to the familiar.

Now and then, Bill caressed me. My leg, my arm, my shoulder, my cheek. He loved me. I loved him. It had taken so long to find him. It had taken so long to find myself.

II.
MAYBE THIS WILL
MAKE ME HAPPY

10. FALLING APART

IN THE FIRST DAYS after that visit to Condon, the tears surprised me in their endless return. When I drove, when I ate, and in bed at night, damp tracks slipping down my face.

In those days after, my breath came only to the top layer of my lungs, small breath, afraid of what I'd find if I took more air in.

I tried to put a name on the pressed-in feeling in my chest, the aching in my stomach. It felt of longing and fear, and I wanted it to go away. The only fix I could imagine was me, pregnant.

The chatter of Mom's words echoed in my head like a herd of running horses. *Missing out. Disappointed. Bitter. Lonely.*

Nothing I did (cry it out, talk to Bill, clean, work, exercise) slowed them. I tried to give them their lead, run them out. I tried to corral them. I tried to forget them. Clean, work, exercise, clean, work, exercise, clean, exercise.

I watched Bill to see if he knew how much I hurt. To see if he would do the fixing thing, say, *Yes, for you I will have a child.*

He did know how much I hurt.

He did not say the fixing thing.

11. THE MAN HE WILL BE

BILL'S FATHER LEFT WHEN Bill was a boy of one, his sister two, his mother about to give birth to another child.

What does a boy learn from a man who leaves his children and his pregnant wife? Who goes far away and comes back two weeks out of the year to take the children on a vacation to fulfill his fatherly duty?

There were hardly any pictures of Bill as a boy. None of him as a baby. Maybe because they were poor. Maybe because the year Bill was a baby was the year his father prepared to leave. No special moments for pictures, no need to recall this hard time.

The one picture I found of him as a little boy I put on a shelf in our living room. Maybe too often I picked up the brass rectangle I'd framed him in, held the cool weight in my hands. Looked at that boy looking at the camera.

It must've been taken a year or two after his father left. Bill and his brother stand side by side in a dusty yard. Their pants are faded, and Bill's are too tight at the waist. He holds his brother's hand.

I look for what's missing, what a staying father could have given. What I see are the features of the man Bill will be. His serious brow, part of him already. His curly hair, part of him already. Maybe the tethers of no-father are part of him already, too, the threads weaving tight, obscuring the lessons another kind of father could have given.

12. THINGS TO DO WHEN I FALL APART

Call a Friend

Pick up the phone. Try not to cry.

Say, "Any chance we can get together?" Talk past the shaky threads in my voice that say what I don't: *Now. Today. I need help.*

Susan heard it in my call, my question, the shake in my voice.

She said, "Meet me tonight. Holiday Market at six." Seven clear words holding a time and place and her, completely there.

This made me want to cry even more.

I got off the phone fast and cried even more.

These new tears were from the asking. And her response. To have someone come when I asked. Right now. Today.

I'd never asked for this kind of help from a friend before. The kind that involved someone seeing me in a mess and not knowing what to do.

Susan and I are just a year apart in age and we share a similar history and sensibility. We were girls raised on Mary Tyler Moore and Lucille Ball. Small-town girls who'd moved to the city.

All the time I'd known Susan, she'd worked full-time and had seemed to like her work. But a year before, when she'd had a baby, she'd given up her job. Now she stayed at home to care for her son. She had plans to have another child. Her husband worked and provided the income. He wanted kids.

I'd admired Susan's life, but I hadn't wanted it. Now, suddenly, what she had looked ideal. Someone like her might say, *Yes! I knew you'd change your mind. Come over to my side. Have a baby. Be a mom! Let's do this together*! But this wasn't why I called her.

Susan had a wide and generous view of the world. She wouldn't try to convince me to join her on the mothering side. She knew how to listen, and she'd be honest with me. I hoped she could help me figure out what to do. One way or the other.

Tell a Friend

The Holiday Market in northeast Portland was an open space with varied booths and vendors selling food. The black-and-white tiled floors echoed with the sound of dishes and silverware and the people at tables. I went past the butcher, the pastry display, the vats of ice cream. I ordered tea and found a table for two.

Susan came with her big smile, her hug. She sat.

I felt raw and scared. I asked about her week. About her son.

Her answers were brief, and then she put her elbows on the table, her chin in her hands. She said, "What's going on?"

People passed by with their coffee and tea and ice cream, bags from the Lloyd Center mall across the street. Voices and footsteps echoed off the floor. The lights were too bright.

I'd thought I was out of tears. I wasn't.

Susan sat in that straight-backed way of hers, head tilted, her eyes on me. I put the tangled-scared-sad-worried-disappointed-confused mess into the space between us.

Her eyes filled with tears when I cried. She didn't try to stop my crying or push a tissue on me, or look around at the people passing by to see if they were staring at this woman with tears running down her face for all to see in the Holiday Market.

"Do you want to stay with Bill?"

"Yes."

"And you're sure he won't change his mind?"

"Yes. And I don't want to push him. I wouldn't want a baby that way. With someone who isn't really into it."

"For you to go so fast from being okay with not having kids to not, based on what your mom said? This is about something more than having a baby."

In that hour, with the backdrop of vanilla scent and the hum of other conversations, Susan took ends of the tangled mess of my wanting, and I took others. We untwisted some of them. The thread of Bill, the thread of family, of work, of child. The thread of my generation that said we women could have it all.

When we finished, I had my hands on the reins, but the herd was still running. The longing hadn't gone away. But now I had this: what it's like to share my hurt with another woman, to feel her hand next to mine as I tried to untangle what was in me. This was new.

Be Held

Cry.

Don't talk about why. We both know why.

Let Bill's hands soothe my back, my hair, my thighs.

Tell him there is nothing he can do.

Tell him I'm not leaving.

Tell him I will be okay. Eventually.

Hope that this is true.

Get Help

Ask around. Get a name. Call her office. Make an appointment.

Days had passed. A week. Two. Even after talking to Susan, I hadn't moved on and snapped back to my easy self. The stampede chatter kept on in my head: *Yes no, why why not, what if what if not, Mom said Bill said, I want don't want, need don't need.*

This was not rational. I couldn't control it. It felt like a grieving. Only no one had died, nothing was lost. Grief for what wasn't. The craving in my gut. Lower. Higher. My womb. My heart.

I'd never been to a counselor before, even though it was my profession. I was the counselor. People came to me for help.

I sat on a couch and she sat on a chair. She had a notepad. I told her why I was there. She didn't take notes.

"I don't know what to do," I said. "What if Mom is right? That I'll end up a bitter, lonely old woman?"

She ran a hand, palm flat, across the yellow notepad. We both watched her hand.

The desk behind her held a tidy stack of files, another notepad, a jar with pens and pencils.

She lifted her eyes to me. "Well," she said, "you better make a decision." Her voice was stern. "Or you'll end up a bitter, lonely old woman." Her hand was still on the blank pad in her lap. "With children."

Everything freeze-frame stopped. The chatter in my mind slowed. Her words held in the air between us as if they were floating. I would come back to these words always.

Bitter.

Lonely.

Old.

With children.

Oh.

I felt smart and dumb all at the same time. I'd been looking here, and the answer was there. The stampede chatter pulled to a halt. Dust rose. Dust settled.

A baby wouldn't keep me from bitter-lonely-old. A baby wouldn't make me special or loved or not a disappointment. It wouldn't give me always-joy. Or make me happy or whole or unhappy or broken or loved or not loved.

What had been in me scattered and came together again in a new form.

I was the one who decided these things.

This would be my touchstone, the logic of my good sense.

BUT MY BODY. It had a logic of its own.

13. IMPORTANT THINGS TO TELL YOUR DAUGHTERS

IN ADDITION TO BIRTH and death, sex was also right outside the picture window on our farm in Condon. To be out in the chicken yard meant seeing a rooster flap his wings and hop on the back of a hen, her contented clucks going screechy under his fast flutter. He jumped off. She high-stepped away, proud-necked and casual as if it hadn't happened in front of all those other hens and whatever of us kids were around. The rooster had already gone on to another.

To look out onto the pasture meant seeing a bull or steer buck up on rear legs and mount another cow. It meant Cris saying, "Look, they're playing piggyback." And me saying, "Yeah," remembering that I'd once thought that too.

I don't know when I knew it was something else, that it was sex and that calves would come in the winter. But I understood what Mom meant to be an adult joke when she and Dad and their friends watched one cow mount another. "It's a real Peyton Place around here," she said. *Peyton Place* was the raciest show on TV, with people kissing the wrong people and sex out of view. All the adults laughed at my smart and funny mom.

But when it came to talking to us girls about these things, Mom's cleverness turned nervous. One afternoon, she stopped Leanne and me as we were passing through the archway between the living and family rooms. I was ten or eleven or twelve. Mom said she wanted to have a talk with us. A talk.

It was a usual afternoon: TV on, boys out doing the chores, Dad gone to town, Cris playing on her own. Mom wasn't acting normal. She pressed her lips tight, and small creases showed up between her eyes. This was not a you-are-in-trouble talk. This was not a lecture or a lesson.

Leanne and I stood side by side, Mom in front of us. Mom spoke in quick words, short sentences. About when you become a woman. Bleeding and pads. Her eyes stayed on us like maybe we should do something, smile or a nod or ask a question, to make it easier for her to say what she felt she had to say right then. About what a man has and what a woman has. How they put these together and babies happen.

They'd already shown us a movie at school. Girls first and then the boys. Cartoon tadpoles going after eggs. A gray-and-black drawing of the twisty tubes in girls like the half-paper paintings we'd done in art: fold the painted side to the unpainted side and press, open it up for a perfect match.

At recess after that movie, not one word was said from a boy to a girl or a girl to a boy. This new knowledge kept us at a constant distance, like the matched poles of magnets, girls by the tetherball, boys out on the softball field.

A girl in my class had already started. She whispered her secret behind the back of her hand to each of us, her news damp in my ear. This new secret of her body meant she knew more than I did.

I'd heard that one girl in grade school had already gone all the way with a high-school boy. The friend who told me about that girl planned to wait until she got married to do it. I said I would too. I thought it would be easy.

Mom told us where the pads and tampons were: in the bathroom in the dresser with the gold pulls.

Maybe Mom's discomfort gave guide to my own feelings. I felt exposed and embarrassed. I looked everywhere but at her.

I said, "Uh-huh," and my sister did too.

I already knew where the pads and tampons were. I knew what to do when I started. I knew about sex. Besides the animals on the ranch and what girls told other girls, I'd had looks at the sexy *Playboy* magazines Dad kept in the cupboard by his easy chair. Pretty women with big breasts and hair between their legs, cartoons of girls with their thighs spread and a man standing between them. I'd read the sexy romance books Mom kept in that cupboard. The covers of these books had dark-haired women held in the arms of handsome men. The man, shiny with sweat and moonlight, leaning into the red lips of the woman, her long black hair trailing down to her waist. Books where men captured women and gave them pleasure. Books with words like *tumescence* and *pulsing* and *throbbing* and *member*.

I went back to those pages with one hand while I touched myself with the other. The ripple wave of that touch moved through my body. Not long after I'd turned eight I learned how good it felt between my legs to climb a pole or a rope. I didn't tell anyone. The secret added to the pleasure.

Now Mom's words sped up like they were trying to find a way out of the room. She said she'd been a virgin with Dad and she was proud of that and we should wait too.

Maybe she worried because a high-school girl was pregnant. Everyone knew about her belly and the baby and the boy who put it there.

Mom said if we didn't wait, we should be careful. We should talk to her. She opened her arms, as though she was pulling back a curtain to show us mothers and daughters who shared personal things.

Then the talk was over, and Mom and Leanne and I and went off to our own things. My relief that it was done must have been Mom's relief too. She never brought it up again. One more thing checked off the list of important things to tell your daughters.

•

AS EACH GIRL IN my class started her period, she whispered it to her friends, who whispered it on. I watched these girls. They made trips to the bathroom with their purses and complained of cramps and sat on the sidelines during gym class. They pretended having a period was something awful. The pain! The blood!

I saw this as bragging, like a race they'd won. No one complained out loud about truly bad things.

Each girl, and her new secret, left me behind. I made my own trips to the bathroom with the slightest hint of a cramp or twinge or damp, and checked for blood. By the end of eighth grade, only me and one other girl in class hadn't started.

Getting your period was like learning to drive or having a boyfriend or drinking alcohol: it's how you knew you were growing up.

Dad kept a 1956 Chevy pickup for us kids to practice driving. I'd been jamming gears and bouncing that pickup over gravel roads since my thirteenth birthday.

I got drunk for the first time in the summer I turned fourteen, on a visit to my Portland cousin. We took sips from the bottles her parents kept in a cupboard, sips small enough not to be missed, large enough for me to see blurry and laugh hard as we ran through the neighborhood, enough to get sick and have to pretend I felt fine the next day.

I'd had a few grade-school boyfriends, nothing more than a ring handed to me by another girl who said, "Rick (or Carl or Steve) wants to go with you." I wanted a boyfriend. I wanted the way it made the other girls seem special and loved and far ahead of me. So I took the ring. But I kept it hidden in a pocket at school, in a drawer at home. Mom would think I was too young for it. I felt too young for it.

We would never talk, the boy and I. One day he would tell his friend, who would tell my friend, who would say to me, "He wants his ring back." Or I'd give it back through that chain of kids, because that boy's pants were too short, or he'd messed up reading out loud in class, or I didn't think he really liked me because we never talked.

I didn't tell any of this to Mom. Not about the boys or drinking and especially not my worry about not having my period. I figured she'd laugh. It wasn't a laughing matter. I felt ashamed of not being part of the woman club.

I never told Leanne either, and she never told me when she got her period. I only knew because she was older and she must have. Plus there was a new box of junior tampons in the dresser drawer.

I felt far behind Leanne even though we were less than two years apart. She had blond hair and a big smile and those blue eyes and a woman's body. My hair was dark and my chest still mostly flat. All the boys liked her even though she had an out-of-town cowboy boyfriend.

I wanted a boyfriend. I wanted to know the secret to getting boys to like me. I was sure happiness would come with a boy.

14. LIKE A BADGE,
LIKE A STAR

I WAITED FOR MY period through the end of grade school and into the summer before my freshman year. I had plenty of time alone that summer.

My brothers and Leanne's boyfriend rode bulls and bareback and saddle broncs at rodeos on summer weekends. Leanne went with her boyfriend. Mom and Dad went as audience and worriers, Cris between them in the grandstands. Each time, Mom asked me if I wanted to go. I said no. I didn't much like rodeos, what they did to the animals. And I liked being alone. The quiet of the house. Long afternoons reading. Books from the library and books from Mom and Dad's cupboard of sex and romance.

Mom had let Leanne and me read her paperback copy of *Valley of the Dolls*, with its racy women and sex and drugs, abortions and affairs, suicide and cancer. I didn't have to hide the reading, but I read the sexy parts alone, again and again. And the opening pages of *The Godfather*. The scene at the wedding, Sonny and the bridesmaid, sex up against a wall. I explored what my body liked, learned the pleasures I could give myself, imagined what else a boy could do for me.

When my family came home, they found me in front of the

TV, or reading a library book. In the same way I never told Mom about my worry about not having my period, I would never tell her about this. The wanting in my body, the yearning and release I could give myself, this woman thing already grown in me, even though I hadn't yet bled.

AT HOME IN THE afternoon, a few weeks into high school, I felt an easing of an ache low in my belly and back. I hadn't known the ache was there until it was gone. A letting go, a warm flow.

I went into the bathroom. The blood in my panties was like a badge, like a star.

I wouldn't be the last girl in class.

The tampons were in the dresser drawer with the gold knobs. I'd studied the directions on the box while I waited for this day. I knew how to use them. I knew my body from touch.

When I left the bathroom, the tampon felt dry in me. I walked and sat carefully, as though it might come out on its own. I sat with my homework and shifted around in my chair and went to the bathroom to make sure the tampon was working okay. Which I could only do by taking it out and putting a new one in. After several trips to the bathroom, each tampon drier than the last, I started to trust that they were working.

AFTER MOM GOT HOME, I waited to tell her. I didn't want it to be a big deal. But not to tell her would be worse, because someday she might ask if I'd started, and she'd know I never told her.

When we were alone, I took a breath and kept my voice steady. "I started my period," I said.

She stopped whatever she was doing, sorting the mail, putting away groceries. "Oh," she said. She turned to me, like there might be something more for us to say about it. Her face was angles of cheekbones and jawline. Whatever excitement I might've had stayed hidden under the shame that it had taken me so long to start. As though it was a personal failing, like not studying hard enough.

She asked me if I needed help with anything and I said no. I felt that tampon in me, imagined the blood flowing past it. I left her and went to the bathroom.

At first the light flow of blood surprised me. By the second day the heavy flow surprised me, and then how many days it went on. I made my own secret trips to the bathroom at school, touched my belly so other girls would know I had cramps. I never told any of them. I'd become a secretive girl over the last few years, and I didn't want to be left behind again.

15. THE MUDDY GROUND

ON THE WAY HOME from school, Bill put his brand-new baseball glove on his hand. He punched the palm of the glove over and over, working the leather, softening it, like the baseball players on TV. He was six or seven, maybe eight. He'd saved up for the glove, penny by penny, nickel by nickel. Odd jobs. Or money from Grandpa. Or maybe it was a special gift. He doesn't remember.

A bigger boy from the neighborhood stopped him. Said, That's my baseball glove you've got there.

Isn't.

Is.

The big boy pushed Bill and Bill fell to the muddy ground.

The big boy ran off. Bill went home: muddy knees, face, seat of pants, hands.

He cried to his mother. Said that boy's name. Said, He pushed me. He took my new glove.

No, Billie, his mother said. Tell the truth. You lost your glove. You were playing in the mud and you lost it.

It wasn't true. But his mother was all he had. No father would come and save them. He was a smart boy.

His mother knew that big boy. She knew of his father. Knew he was the kind of man who taught his son to take and fight.

Maybe this is why she didn't believe her son. She didn't have enough power in her or enough power behind her to face that man.

Bill tells me that story. He says, "I understood right then, she had to say that. What could she do? It was better for her to think it was my fault. I even started to think it was my fault."

Wouldn't the man who had been this bullied boy want to have his own child? To heal that wound. Teach him how to stand up against bullying power.

No. It doesn't work that way.

Maybe this man worries he might be like the mother who doesn't believe the child's story. Or maybe he worries he might be like the father who isn't there.

16. CLEARLY, BOLDLY, NO APOLOGIES

IN THE MONTHS AFTER the longing for a child rose up so strong in me, I worked to make peace with it. To carry on as I'd planned and be happy with all that I had: my life with Bill, friends, travel, work, time with nieces and nephews. I was intent on finding my way back to the easy joy I'd known before.

I didn't tell any other friends about my struggle. They might pity me, or judge Bill. They might try to push my longing further than it had already gone. So I kept my struggle to myself.

My friend Bonnie would have been the logical one to reaffirm my decision to not have children. I kept thinking of her, and a conversation we'd had over lunch not long before I met Bill.

She'd been one of my closest friends. We'd worked together for a few years but, by the time of that lunch, we'd taken different jobs in different parts of town, and now our contact was only a quick hour every month or so.

We sat at a wooden booth at McCormick's that day and caught up, talked of her work and mine. Gossip of friends in common. The breakup of her last relationship.

Both of us started in on our salads, tiny pink shrimp curled on top.

Then, in a casual way, she said, "I'm getting my tubes tied next week."

I about dropped my fork.

We'd never talked about kids. I assumed she wanted them, like I assumed every woman did, and would have them when the right time came. But here she was, taking a bite of her salad like she'd just told me a plan to buy another beat-up old Mustang, something she did occasionally and later had to put way too much money into.

She looked up at me, how still I'd gone. She raised her pale eyebrows. "What?" she said.

I leaned in toward her. "Why?" I said, ready to talk her out of it.

"I've always been pretty sure I didn't want kids. Now I am for *sure* sure," she said. "I don't want to bring a kid into this world." Clearly, boldly, no apologies.

Bonnie was funny and bright and shining. I'd seen her with my nieces and nephew on a visit we all took to the zoo. She'd made them laugh and follow her. She'd be a wonderful mother.

I started in about how she might change her mind. She was so young, still in her twenties. She might meet someone who wanted a baby. I told her how I used to really want kids and, even though now I thought I'd be okay without them, I still saw it as a possibility.

"Wait a while," I said. "It's so final. What if you change your mind?"

"I won't." She wasn't asking for my advice or opinion. She had a plan, no approval needed.

She said this world wasn't a place she wanted to bring a kid into. She said she didn't have the maternal instinct. Birth control was too iffy. She knew what she was doing.

Bonnie made her own decisions and acted on them. Her mom had died when Bonnie was in her teens. Her dad was an alcoholic and he lived on the streets. She was distant from her sister and brother. She'd learned a long time ago not to look for anyone's help or approval.

She carried the full weight of her survival on her own. I had no idea what that would be like. I could turn to my family if I needed help with food or money or a place to live. This was a fortune and a privilege I'd never been as aware of before that day.

But Bonnie's aloneness also meant she didn't need to worry about the expectations and disappointment of others. Expectations of mothers and fathers. Disappointments I didn't even know the power of yet.

The next time I saw Bonnie, she'd had the surgery. We never talked about it again. I couldn't understand the finality of her choice and I wondered if she'd regret it.

Bonnie moved to Hawaii not long after that. Aside from the occasional cards back and forth, and a lavish bouquet of flowers she sent the day Bill and I got married, we mostly lost contact.

In the first year after the longing opened up in me and for years beyond that, I thought back to that lunch. Bonnie's choice became a touchstone for me. I used it to understand Bill's clarity about not wanting a child.

Some people grow up in a way that smothers the parenting urge. Or maybe they never have it. Maybe I needed to consider that this was as normal as having the urge. Why should a person automatically want a child? Why should that be the normal thing? As Mom's disappointment settled in me, I felt ashamed of the way I'd tried to talk Bonnie out of her choice.

I used the touchstone of her to find comfort in my own plan to not have a child. Bonnie was out there doing what I was doing, being childfree. She must be happy with her decision.

I could have called her for reassurance. But I didn't. In the same way I didn't want to be talked out of my decision to not have a child, I also didn't want to be talked into it.

17. LIKE I KNEW
WHAT I WAS DOING

GRADE SCHOOL WAS FOR pretend boyfriends. In high school you got the real thing. By the summer before my sophomore year, the two most popular girls in class had boyfriends, even a couple of the quiet girls had rings from older boys, and Leanne still had her out-of-town cowboy boyfriend.

I met my first real boyfriend at a rodeo dance late in the summer, right after I turned fifteen. He had blond hair and blue eyes. He rode bulls in rodeos and was lean and a little bowlegged. He picked me out of the handful of girls without dates and asked me to dance. He wore his cowboy hat at a tilt, and for seventeen he was cocky and sure of himself. The moment he turned his blue eyes toward me, I let go of my thoughts about what rodeos did to animals. I would do anything to get him. To keep him.

He danced the Western Swing with me and made it look like I knew what I was doing. At the end of the night he asked for my phone number. Not long after that, he called and came for a visit. Now I had my very own out-of-town cowboy.

BEFORE SCHOOL STARTED THAT year, Mom and Dad took Cris and me on a weekend trip to Pendleton.

"It'll be a vacation," Mom said.

"There'll be a swimming pool at the motel," Dad said.

"You're coming," they both said.

Mom and Dad would want to go out on a Saturday night in Pendleton and they needed me to be the babysitter. Cris was seven and couldn't be left in a motel room alone. Pat was married and gone from home by then, and Leanne and Brad had summer jobs and didn't have to come on this trip.

Things had changed in our family in a way that I wouldn't have been able to name back then, maybe because it had come on so gradually. It was a kind of breaking apart, some of which was to be expected from us kids getting older and going our own ways. But, more than that, the ulcer problems Mom had over the years had gotten worse and she didn't have the energy she used to have for mothering or paying attention to what we were up to. And Dad's drinking took him away from us more and more. Most nights we put his dinner in the oven on warm-bake and were heading off to bed by the time he came home.

I'd pulled back from expecting too much from either of my parents, which helped to keep me from any disappointment. So I might have protested against going on this weekend vacation in Pendleton. But I didn't. I thought it might be fun, the four of us together. I liked watching out for my little sister. And I liked swimming in motel pools. Best of all, my cowboy boyfriend lived closer to Pendleton than he did to Condon, and he said he'd come to see me.

On the Saturday of our vacation, Cris and I played in the motel pool most of the afternoon. Neither Mom nor Dad came down to jump in or to watch us. After a while, Dad came out and said he was going out for a bit and that Mom had a headache and needed to rest. He didn't say where he was going. I knew he'd find a bar.

The sun went behind the roof of the motel. Cris and I went to our room and changed out of our suits and then to Mom's room. We all walked over to Cimmiyotti's Steak House, a fancy restaurant near the motel. We'd meet Dad there.

The light was low in the restaurant. The young waiter, not much older than me, led us to the table. Candles put shadows on the ceiling and the white tablecloths.

Mom kept looking toward the dark doorway that led to the bar. The candles made shadows under her eyes and in the hollows under her cheekbones. The waiter took our orders for our drinks, Mom, Cris, me: just water, Shirley Temple, Coke.

Dad came out of the bar, slow, careful in his steps. He stood next to the waiter. His face was loose and empty with alcohol. "And a gin and tonic," Dad said to the waiter. The top of him moved in a swaying circle. One hand held the chair.

The menu in my hand was heavy with the idea of food I hadn't ordered, didn't want anymore.

The waiter put a hand on Dad's elbow and pulled the chair out. Dad sat with a slump, one of his arms on the table, the other gone slack over his knee.

"Yes, sir. A gin and tonic." The waiter backed up. He looked at me, fast and away. I pressed the crease in the white tablecloth.

Mom put her hand across her forehead, holding her temples. "Jesus, Jack." Two quiet words, swinging for a fight. The tension between them had become familiar in the past few years. Him drinking, her mad.

The disappointment came down on me, the dark weight of it. How drunk he was. He could have come swimming with us like he used to when the whole family went to the beach for a week-long vacation after harvest. He could have had the afternoon of doing something fun; we could all be here like a regular family instead of a family pretending he wasn't drunk, that Mom wasn't angry. It burned in me, my stomach, my chest, my throat.

Dad leaned into the arm on the table. His other arm came up slow, careful. He rested one hand on the other. Cris was pressed back in her chair, almost disappeared in the dim light.

Dad's eyelids hovered low. "What're you girls having to eat?" He blinked a few hard blinks, as if he wasn't drunk, as if

Mom wasn't there with her eyes covered and her jaw clenched up tight.

It was a still-frame moment, and inside this moment my voice came through the burn of my throat. I said, "Oh Dad." I slid out of my chair and left the table. Took the words that could hurt him, past the table, past the candles, the waiter with our drinks.

"Babe," Dad called out, "come back." Surprised.

Mom said, "Let her go." I couldn't tell if her raised voice was for him or for me.

I pushed open the glass doors of the restaurant and stepped out into the late summer night. I'd never walked away from either of them before. I'd never not come when they called.

The warm summer air tasted of dried grass and dust. My boyfriend's phone number was in my back pocket on a slip of paper he'd given me, but I'd already memorized it. I walked toward the motel room, swung the key from the black oval tag that was so big it could never be lost.

By the time Mom came with Cris, the cowboy was with me, him sitting on the bed, me perched on the edge of a chair because I knew Mom would be bringing Cris to the room we were sharing. Mom asked if I was okay. The cowboy watched. I hadn't told him about Dad. I kept my back straight and my jaw tight. I said yes, I was okay.

Mom said to the cowboy, "You'll have to leave by ten o'clock." She looked at me, her belief that I would be a good girl held in the way she nodded at me before she went out the door.

Cris sat on the floor in front of the lit TV screen. The cowboy pulled me over next to him on the bed. He kissed me. Cris turned and looked at us. Then looked back at the TV.

The cowboy tried to get me to lie down on the bed with him. "I can't," I said. Shadows of TV people in the dark room. The silhouette of Cris from behind. I wanted to be a good girl.

18. RED DAYS CIRCLED

IN THE FRONT SEAT of his white Pontiac LeMans, I told my cowboy boyfriend, "I want to." When I unbuttoned my pants for him, I said yes. "Yes," when he asked was I sure. He'd already been my boyfriend for a month.

Sex was nothing like in the books. Nothing like what I did for myself when I was alone. It was fast and quiet and I didn't feel much of anything other than the armrest pressing in my back, the cool of the red vinyl seat, the relief that I hadn't waited any longer to have this secret of my own.

Afterward he said, "Are you sure you didn't do this before? You sure seem to know what you're doing."

I SAT ON THE bleachers before volleyball practice. I touched thumb to fingers, counted days. A week late. The other girls came out of the locker room and started hitting practice serves and sets. I put my elbows to my knees, chin to hand.

The cowboy and I had been together three months and we'd had sex plenty of times since that first time. He didn't like to use condoms. It didn't feel good. I told him that was okay. I knew when I could get pregnant.

I could tell when an egg was there. On those days I had a small headache and felt a fullness in me. I knew how long to wait on either side of that headache. I'd read a book that said there were spermicides and condoms and now there was the Pill. I didn't know how to get any of those. The book said what I was doing was old fashioned. But it had worked so far. Until now.

I'd seen that girl who got pregnant in high school. The older women cooed and held her child. That girl was a pale thing next to her shining baby.

I wouldn't have a baby. And Mom couldn't know I'd been this dumb. More than once over the years Mom said to me, "You may be smart, but you have no common sense." I never asked her exactly what she meant by that, but I figured it had to do with thinking things through beyond a first thought or an idea or a want.

My friends on the volleyball court called to me, "C'mon, Shannon! Get down here and start hitting some balls." And they laughed. Shoes squeaked on the shiny gym floor. The slap of open palms on volleyballs.

I pictured a calendar in my mind. Red days circled. The rhythm of my body. My periods always came when they should.

I wouldn't tell my cowboy boyfriend. Not now. Maybe not ever. In the months since that first time in his white LeMans, he went from gentle boy to one who wanted sex whenever we were alone. He said it hurt if we didn't. On the days I thought I could get pregnant, he showed me how to do something else. Use my hand or use my mouth.

Everyone at school, the teachers and the other kids, thought I was a good girl. They had no idea how much time the cowboy and I spent on back roads.

I forgot how to say no to him. This became a habit, me not saying no. Maybe this was how it was. Maybe all the girls stopped saying no once they had said yes.

My boyfriend talked about us getting married. He said his mom had been fifteen when she married his dad. She was a nice lady, but I saw her life. Staying at home, hardly any friends, a husband who told her what to do.

I didn't say yes and didn't say no when the cowboy said

marriage. Mom was already talking to me about college and careers. I didn't tell the cowboy that I wanted what Mom wanted for me.

How could I want a boy to love me so much but not want to be with him forever?

If I was pregnant, someone would help me figure it out, tell me where to go. Help make it go away. I'd read *Valley of the Dolls*, seen that TV show *Maude*. From the little bit of news I paid attention to, I knew abortion was legal now. For sure there were girls I could ask for help.

Smart came from learning things from books. Common sense would have kept this from happening in the first place.

The coach blew her whistle. I got off the bleachers and pulled up my knee pads. I powered my serves and dove for wild balls. If I could knock it loose, I would. If it was there.

THREE MORE DAYS WENT by. I tried not to think about what might be growing in me. I didn't tell my boyfriend. The worry settled in with an ache low in my back. I didn't want to marry him.

The ache rested heavy and low and I didn't recognize it until two more days passed. Then came the rush of blood. A different kind of release than the first time I had bled. I breathed it in. I hadn't told anyone, so I had no one to tell my relief to.

I STRETCHED OUT THE days on either side of those headaches, the days I counted when the egg might be there. Sometimes I wasn't careful and hoped it would be okay.

The cowboy told me what to wear and what I couldn't wear when he wasn't around. He didn't want me talking to other boys. He said my short haircut made my nose look even bigger. He said I was getting fat. A friend told me my boyfriend had gone out with another girl.

At first, I tried to keep him without ever thinking whether I wanted him anymore. I missed the way it had been at first, the excitement of falling in love. My boyfriend didn't seem to know the sex should be for me too.

I missed how it felt when I wanted to do anything for him, when I would do anything for him.

YEARS LATER, WHEN WE became the kind of sisters who talked about such things, Leanne said she'd waited until she was eighteen and had moved out of Mom and Dad's house. She said she didn't think it was right, not respectful to our parents, to do it before then. She'd thought it through so clearly. She had rules about what was right and what was wrong. How did she know that? How did I not?

19. ANOTHER THING TO DO WHEN I FALL APART

Clear the Air

About a month after that visit to Condon, I told Bill I wanted to visit again.

As with many kinds of grief, I looked for the thing that would take me back to before the loss had begun. Even though the wildness of my feelings had begun to settle, the hooves of Mom's words kept kicking at me. Disappointed. Lonely. Bitter. These words knocked loose my sense of purpose and direction and jolted the confidence I'd had in my relationship with Bill.

I wanted Mom to make it better.

Over the weekend with my family, I waited until late on Saturday night, after dinner and after my brothers and sisters and their sleepy kids had gone home. Waited until Dad and Bill had gone to bed.

Once again, Mom and I were alone in the family room, TV turned down low. She hovered a pencil over a crossword puzzle. I sat on the sofa doing nothing more than trying to find the right words to begin.

My family didn't admit when we were hurt. We didn't let go of a hurt by talking about it to the one who let loose the arrow. Talking might make everything worse. I didn't want to hurt Mom by telling her she had hurt me. And I didn't want that hurt turned back on me.

She tilted her head to the paper, fitting letters into squares.

My beating heart that had once beat inside her.

I took a breath. "Mom," I said.

"Hmmm?" She penciled another letter on the page.

"You know last time we were here?"

"Uh-huh." The light of the lamp made a shiny gold circle on her dark hair.

"What you said about me not having children?"

She looked up, pencil above gridded letters. "What did I say?"

How could she forget? How could she not have felt tangled up in the mess I'd been carrying for the last month?

"You said you were worried." The words were shaky in me. "That I'd end up being a bitter, lonely old woman."

She widened her eyes. Surprised. "Oh," she said. Her eyes changed to remembering. "I did say that, didn't I?"

I started to cry.

She put the paper and pencil on the table.

"I felt really bad about it," I said. "I'm happy with Bill. We're not having kids. I didn't decide that randomly."

"Oh, Jackie." Her voice wavered. "I didn't mean." Soft. Careful.

"I want you to be proud of me." I said I'd followed her push, gone to college, gotten a degree. That maybe I'd had some wrong starts, but I had a good career. Bill was the right man for me.

I wanted her to say she saw this. To take back her hurtful words. I wanted what I'd always wanted from her. For her to approve of me.

"I *am* proud of you." She sat up straighter. "We're both proud of you. For all that. College. Work." She leaned forward. "But more than that. Who you are. What you do for our family. You bring us together. Bill too. I can tell how happy you are with him."

"I've felt . . ." A careful search for the right word. "I don't know. Mad. I guess. And hurt."

My words made her cry. They made me cry.

"I only meant I'll miss having more grandkids," she said. "And being a mother has been my biggest joy." She went on fast, like she was trying to reach me, to give me what I needed. "But that doesn't mean your life isn't wonderful. That I don't think it is. You're doing things I never will."

She wiped her eyes, her nose. We looked at each other. I still sat on the sofa and she still sat in her chair, but the distance between us had narrowed.

Not gone, just less.

She couldn't take her words back, even if she tried. I'd already absorbed them into me. The childfree life I'd been so sure of had taken a wound, and I would never be so sure again.

I didn't tell her this. She might use it as proof of her rightness. She might worry about my happiness, the thing a mother most wants for her girl. That worry might lead her to open the wound even more.

I thanked her for listening. I told her I loved her. Again I was aware of my heart beating as she went back to her crossword and I went into the bathroom to get ready for bed.

She had taken a wound too. She'd had other yearnings: for college or art or medicine, but she came from a generation that hardly gave her any choice at all.

A child living the kind of life the parent chose is a validation of that life. Me having a child would have been a validation of the wild and messy years Mom had gone through raising us five kids.

I'd given her plenty of reasons to worry in the years from my teens to my early twenties. Since then, I'd been working to prove to her that all that hard work as a mother, and all my exploring as a teenager, had been worth it. Me having a child would be the kind of balancing that is important between mothers and daughters.

20. GET A GLOW ON

I ENDED THINGS WITH my cowboy boyfriend in the middle of junior year by getting into the back seat of a car with another boy and letting the cowboy find out, not from me, but from the way stories were whispered from ear to ear, about girls in back seats of cars.

After that new boy, word got around. More boys asked me out. They took me for a drive. I kept up my habit of not saying no.

In a small town, with a high school of not much more than a hundred kids, it's possible to be many things. I was a popular girl, Honor Society president, an actor in every school play, the girl friends came to with their problems. I was the dance team leader, a setter on the volleyball team, a princess at the prom. And I was a slut. I excelled.

The boys I gravitated to were the older ones, most of them already graduated from high school. They smoked pot and partied and knew things about cities and music and drugs and the world. Things I thought I should know. Things I wanted to know.

Each time with each new boy that first urge and pull, the hot breathlessness, flamed possibility that this boy could do for me what I did for myself when I was alone: bring pleasure and relief. The possibility he could give me love and I could give it to him, that we could go on like that, romance under the moonlight. In the back seat of a car. But that didn't happen. They were boys. They knew even less than I knew.

SOME GIRLS HAD SERIOUS boyfriends. Girls already planning to marry after high school, to stay in Condon, start a family. This was not my plan. This was not Mom's plan. She'd been talking about college since my sophomore year; talking about it like it the idea came from me, something that would happen, not a question. Talking about it long enough that I did think it was my idea. This is where Mom focused her attention. She saw to it that I made it home by curfew, kept up with my grades, did my chores. She didn't know about all those boys. All those back seats.

ONE NIGHT, LATE IN my senior year, I drove home from a party, whiskey and beer and cigarettes and boy on me. I took the highway slow and careful and drunk, and went even slower at the turnoff to our ranch, up the gravel road. The lights of the house blurred in the distance.

Mom would be awake as she was always awake, waiting for her family to come home. But the older kids were grown and gone. Cris was still a child, already in bed. Dad was out at the bar like he was most nights while she waited, while I waited, while we all waited. While we looked for his lights in the driveway, felt the disappointment when he finally came home, drunk and distant. She had stopped waiting for him; he'd be home sometime. I was the only one left to wait for.

I parked in the driveway. Turned the engine off. Mom there in her chair in the lamp-lit picture window. TV flicker. I got out slow and careful. Held myself on car door, hood of car. Steadied on the picket fence, breathed whiskey breath, up the sidewalk on legs like bendy straws, up the porch steps.

I came in the front door and stood there, slack-eyed. Mom

had a pad of thick art paper on her lap, calligraphy pens spread out around her. Some old movie on TV.

"Hi," I said, the thick drunk of it in my throat.

She looked me up and down. "Hi," she said.

This was where Dad stood, all those nights when he finally came home, his dinner dried up in the oven.

Mom looked at the clock.

I looked at the clock. Squinted my eyes. It was one a.m. Just on time.

He'd ask us what we learned at school that day. Stand there, the top of him making small swaying circles. We gave one-word answers. Fine. Okay. Good. Knowing he wouldn't remember in the morning.

I started past her to go to the bathroom. My shoulder bumped the wall, and I caught myself there, looked to see if she saw.

She sat up straighter. "Are you drunk?"

I stood up tall. "No," I said. Tried to hold my eyes steady on hers. Like that would prove it.

Her eyes didn't move from me. "You are," she said.

"I am not," I said.

She looked back at the paper in front of her. Rows of practice calligraphy letters, curvy lines and swirls. "It's not good for a girl to get drunk." Her innocence floated in the air between us. "It's not ladylike." She said it like another mother-daughter talk, one she'd forgotten. "You're only supposed to get a glow on. A drink or two," she said, "to feel happy. That's all. Otherwise it's sloppy. And ugly." A last chance for her to teach me. A last chance for me to listen.

She picked up her pen. She drew slow inky lines on the thick paper, and the paper took that ink in.

21. WE'LL TALK ABOUT THIS LATER

IN THE SPRING OF my senior year, Mom smiled a hopeful smile when I asked if she and Dad would be chaperones for the high school prom.

"I was voted princess," I said.

"Your dad will be tickled you asked." Her smile went bigger. "It'll be fun." As though we were that kind of family, the kind that shared everything.

On the night before prom, I left the pink satin dress I'd made in home ec hanging on the coat closet door. The pattern was sexy, like an old-fashioned movie star. It showed off my strong shoulders, my slim waist. Mom said it was pretty but to leave it downstairs so she could iron it.

The next morning Mom pointed at the dress, neatly ironed of all creases. "I got to looking at your sewing on that. The seams were a little loose." She'd stayed up late resewing every seam. "I was worried it would come apart when you dance."

I felt ashamed. I felt angry. My poor work, her need to point it out, her need to fix it.

I'm sure I didn't thank her.

•

MY DATE AND I wandered into the prom over an hour late, steps fluid with alcohol, eyes wide on speed. The pink satin dress was creased and the hem dirty with mud from the back road we'd been on, drinking and making out.

The crowning ceremony was over. Another girl was the queen.

Mom and Dad stood at the back of the room with the other chaperones. Arms folded, eyes narrow. I pretended I didn't see they were mad, took my date's hand, and went over to them. Like I could make up for it, the way I was embarrassing them in front of the other parents, the teachers, their own hope that I was a better girl. I said, "Oh, sorry. We lost track of time." And I laughed.

Their tight faces, their mouths in straight lines holding words they wouldn't say because this was public and they wouldn't embarrass themselves any more than I already had.

I nudged Mom toward my date. "C'mon Mom, dance with him and I'll dance with Dad."

Mom pulled at my arm. "Where were you?"

Dad ran his hand over his face and said to Mom, "Jeanie, we'll talk about this later." He was completely sober. "We don't want to dance," he said.

My date and I moved away, and I stayed on the far side of the room, pretending prom was fun, not looking their way, not wanting to see my reflection in them, how thoughtless I was.

DAWN LIGHT MADE SHADOWS in the family room when I came in the front door. Prom was long over.

"You're late." The silhouette of Dad in his chair.

I stayed by the door, my hand on the knob.

"I know."

That sexy satiny dress had done its job and held together. Now it was wadded up in the back seat where I'd fallen asleep with my date. I wore the old jeans and a T-shirt I kept for backup.

"Come here," Dad said.

His disappointment was like something I could touch. It made his eyes soft and pressed his shoulders down. It filled the air as I moved toward him. I thought I might cry. He took my hand and pulled me down onto his lap. I hadn't been in his lap since I was a little girl. Faint memory of cupping my hands over the stubble on his chin, my head against his chest, my feet barely reaching his knees.

Now I kept my body stiff and upright and awkward. My legs next to his, feet on the floor, his hand around my shoulder. Would he smell the sex on me, the cigarettes?

"You've gotten so grown-up," he said. He put his arms around me, and I relaxed a little. I leaned into him. For one sweet moment I was his brown-eyed girl again. It had been so long since either he or Mom had touched me or held me. And for that moment, I felt his love and his loss and mine.

The old mantel clock ticked, the shadows in the room faded.

And then it felt awkward and false, a thing whose time had passed. I sat up, and Dad eased his hold. He touched my chin, turning it so that our eyes met. "You embarrassed your mother tonight," he said. "I'm disappointed in you."

Some things are easier to know, without the words. Hearing them out loud came with a weight. His disappointment. All those nights I'd waited for him to come home. I could have felt glad for him to know what it was like. Him drunk, me waiting. But he was the father. I was the daughter.

"Get your car keys," he said. "You're not driving that car for a week."

I almost laughed at the smallness of it, after what I'd done, after all I'd been doing. I stood up, stiff-backed, went to my purse and found the keys to the Nova, and gave them to him. He nodded and put them in his pocket. "One week," he said.

I never had to ask Mom or Dad for a ride. I never had to take the school bus. I never said I was sorry. My friends or one of those boys came to pick me up before school and dropped me off after. The shame I felt at disappointing my parents faded in the dust of those cars coming up our gravel road, and I kept on with my wild ways.

22. THE LAST THING TO DO WHEN I FALL APART

Find Comfort, Give Comfort

Bill had stayed awake waiting for me after my talk with Mom. The lamp on the nightstand lit the silver in his hair.

During the weeks of my sudden turn from not wanting a baby to wanting one, Bill hadn't gotten angry with me, not for one moment, even though I was the one who wanted to change the rules. He'd been quiet, watchful. He'd already had one marriage with a wife who wanted more than he could give.

"How'd it go?" he said, because he knew I'd planned to have this conversation with Mom.

"It went okay." I got into bed. "I'm glad I talked to her."

"Good." He put his hand on my thigh. His palm was warm and strong, a comfort.

The sound of the TV came up through the vent. Mom would be down there in her chair, pencil hovered over her crossword, flicker shadow of light and dark across her face.

Bill said, "How are you feeling about things now?" That question held all the questions he didn't ask: Would I stay? Would I keep loving him? Would I try to push, threaten, bully him into having a child? Didn't I see that even though he didn't want a child he wanted everything else with me?

I turned my whole body to him. "Don't worry." I looked in his eyes. "I'll be all right. We'll get through this."

He held his eyes on mine, looking for the truth in what I said.

I leaned past him and turned off the lamp. "Good night," I said.

I turned onto my back and looked up at the grid shadow made by the light coming through the vent on the floor, breathed the dust and memories of my old bedroom. I wished I could go back to the way I'd been before, when I didn't have this burden of my wanting.

23. THIS IMPORTANT WEIGHT

BILL'S FAMILY GATHERED AROUND the table as they often gathered around the table during his childhood. Food, talk, cards. Always, this family played cards. Mother, aunts, uncles. Sister and brother nearby. No father.

Bill stood by the table, just tall enough to see the cards dealt around. *Tick, tick, tick.* He was three or four or five. Learning numbers, learning shapes: diamond, heart, club, spade. Learning language: trick, bid, lead, fold.

An uncle put his hand on Bill's shoulders. Said, *You're the man of the house now.*

Three or four or five. Old enough to remember. Old enough to take it in. The boy stretches up, presses into the weight of the hand. He presses himself into this new role.

Over the years, his shoulders curve and slope with the weight. Problem solver, go-to son, brother, nephew.

Man of the house.

He carries this important weight all the way through childhood. Carries it still.

24. SHINY BOWS OF BLUE AND SILVER

THE WOMEN OF CONDON gave three showers in the months before I graduated high school. One for a girl in my class who was marrying the boy she'd dated since she was a freshman. One for Pat's wife, expecting their first child. And one for Leanne, who was marrying her cowboy boyfriend.

Leanne's shower took place in the Demonstration Hall at the fairgrounds. The hostesses decorated the room with Leanne's wedding colors in blue crepe paper and silver bells. Bowls of pastel mints and mixed nuts were set out on long folding tables.

Leanne sat at the head table. As her maid of honor, I had the place of honor next to her. Mom and Cris, Nana, and the mother of Leanne's future husband also shared the table.

Women brought gifts wrapped in thick paper with shiny bows of silver and blue. Leanne unwrapped present after present after present. She was careful with the bows because each one that broke meant a child would be born of the marriage. Cris collected and gathered the bows into a fake bouquet for Leanne to carry at the wedding rehearsal. I made a list of gift and giver: Stoneware place setting. Set of blue towels. Crystal pickle bowl.

Leanne's new layered hair cut framed her face. She was beautiful. She admired each item: candlesticks, a vase, a hand mixer, measuring cups and spoons, and thanked each woman.

She would have a husband. She would have a home. She was nineteen years old.

We were different, my sister and I. Not just her blond hair and blue eyes against my dark hair and brown eyes. She had a future she was sure of, and a purity next to my secrets and longings.

The hangover still hung on me from the night before, mixed with the memory of the boy I'd been with. My desire to leave this town had grown strong even though I had no idea about the kind of life I wanted.

The women talked and sipped coffee, tea, punch. The mints disappeared and the mixed nuts trickled down to a few peanuts in each bowl. Many of these women had already been married by the time they were nineteen; some already had babies by that age. This celebration brought back their own memories and drew an approving line under their own choices.

The opened gifts were passed for each woman to look at, to touch, to talk with one another about.

"Oh, how pretty."

"I'd like one of these."

"Isn't her china pattern lovely?"

The hostesses stacked the gifts in the corner. Cake was cut and served, more tea and coffee poured. Leanne stood up and thanked the hostesses and the women of town. She introduced me, her maid of honor, and Cris, her bridesmaid, even though everyone already knew us.

She told about where she and Larry would live after they married. Mom looked at her and smiled, Nana's chin lifted with a grandmother's pride. Aunt Lena sat at a table with all the other women, not at the table of honor. Her thick glasses reflected the faces of the women in the room, smiling and nodding and welcoming Leanne into the world of woman things.

•

LEANNE'S WEDDING WAS ON a Saturday afternoon at the Church of Christ. Before the ceremony, in the Sunday school room, Cris and I stood nearby and watched Mom help Leanne with her dress and arrange her veil.

Leanne and Mom moved quietly together, womanly and calm, like they were continuing a conversation they'd started when I wasn't paying attention. A wife and a soon-to-be wife.

Nana sat nearby, holding Pat's first child, a daughter. Tawna had been born the month before. Nana looked even prouder than she'd been at Leanne's wedding shower. Her first great-grandchild.

Being an aunt for the first time was cool. But my interest in the baby had a short duration. I was seventeen! I was about to graduate high school! There was a wedding and I was in it!

When the music started, Cris went down the aisle in the hesitation steps we'd practiced the night before. Then I went down the aisle. The music lifted, and Leanne and Dad came. Her hand on his arm. Him looking proud in his fine suit, his blond-haired girl next to him.

Leanne's almost-husband in his powder-blue suit waited for her at the altar, hands folded in front of him. She'd wanted him all through her high school years, and now chose him for the rest of her life. Years later she would tell me she knew the minute she met Larry that he would be a good father.

I'd never thought that far ahead when it came to boys. I never thought how this boy or that might fit into my future, or considered what he could do beyond make me fall for him for a while.

THERE WERE NO SHINY bows or cake for my graduation a week after Leanne's wedding. But gifts came anyway, from relatives and the people of Condon. Gifts for a girl going away to college: laundry bags and towels, stationery with postage stamps, envelopes of money. Notes saying congratulations and good luck with my future.

College was the thing for me. "You've got the smarts," Mom had been saying for the past three years. "You're going."

I'd chosen a social work program in Eugene, a five-hour drive away from home, in a town Mom said was full of hippies and druggies. She worried about how that would combine with my lack of common sense. But she didn't try to change my mind.

Even if the big celebrations were about babies and weddings, I thought would make Mom proud. I would be the first child of hers to get a four-year degree.

25. HIS PLACE OF BETTER SUNSETS

EVERY MONTH OR SO, Bill and I took the three-hour drive east along the Columbia River, then south from Biggs, through Wasco and on to Condon. About twenty miles from town, the land and sky open up to rolling hills speckled with sagebrush, fields of powder soil, wheat and mountains in the distance.

In the year after the child-wanting in me set in, going back to Condon was like a relief valve. It didn't make sense that I looked forward to going to the place that had ignited my confusion about motherhood. But as we got closer to town, my jaw relaxed and the tightness in my chest eased.

Between Bill's siblings and mine, we now had twelve nieces and nephews. I'd held each of the five on my side from the first months of their lives, and the connection since that first holding ran deep. Going to Condon meant time with them. These weekends were full of hard playing and child holding. And a chance to show my parents that I'd chosen the right man in Bill, that I was happy in my life, that these kids were enough. It was a chance to show myself this too.

On one of the drives home, I felt a surge of love for this land as wide open as the view in front of us. I said to Bill, "This place has the best skies. The best sunsets. No trees or buildings in the way. The sunsets here are more beautiful than anywhere."

These were the sunsets of my memory, from before I left this place intent on being a girl from somewhere else.

Bill smiled his knowing smile. "I know a place that has sunsets that will blow your mind. Better than here even."

A sharpness came up in me. "Why do you have to say there's something better?" Picking a fight. The skies here flowed from pink to orange to darkest purple.

"Jackie," Bill said, slow and careful, stepping back from the edge in my voice. "I'm just saying I'd like to show you this other place."

I was trying to tell him something that was a feeling, not a truth. Why couldn't he see the beauty here?

WHEN WE LEFT CONDON after a weekend, waved goodbye to my family standing on the porch, my sadness about leaving melded into a surge of longing. My questions started.

"Are you sure you don't want kids?"

"Are you still sure?"

"How can you be so sure?"

As though this could wear away his not wanting.

His answers never changed.

"Yes."

And "Yes."

And "I just am."

I couldn't understand. He loved our nieces and nephews. He could play and chase and goof, stick a grape up his nose and get it stuck and make them laugh so hard they almost wet their pants. He could pick up a child with me (*you take the hands, I take the legs*) and swing one-two-three. How could a man like this not want a child of his own?

BILL TOOK ME TO his place of better sunsets. We drove in his black Saab, pulling our small tent trailer to the desert of southern Utah. Capitol Reef, Zion, Bryce, Arches.

Sometimes when Bill was driving, I watched him. His profile: strong nose, curls curving the back of his head, this angle of him. Even here, I asked, "Are you still sure?" As though he would suddenly be struck with something new, something that hadn't struck him for all of his more than forty years. That he would slap his forehead and say, *Oh, wait a minute, I was wrong, I do want children.*

But he didn't say that. His shoulders slumped, curved in, the weight and pressure of my wanting wore on him. "I'm still sure," he said. He sounded tired.

I looked at the land around us. Here too, the skies were wide open. But this was another place. Canyons carved by glaciers and floods. A great basin once underwater. Uplifts formed by thrusts and folds and colliding plates.

There were no faults in Bill's story. When a pregnant woman was in the room, his eyes never followed her like mine did. He never said how gorgeous she was with her round belly, her secret smile. When an infant was passed, he never held out his arms. I'd never seen him hold a baby. He didn't question a new father about what it was to like to be a new father.

We hiked early in the mornings, before the big heat, hiked in the scent of sand and creosote, cottonwood seed floating in the air. We hiked sand drifts that had petrified to hardened dune, no trail visible except for cairns that marked the way on the slickrock. Slick. Rock. Solid, yet slippery from the fine sand dusting it.

We returned to camp in the afternoon, sated from sun and hike. Found a shower, had a nap, made love.

There, as at home, sex never mixed with the possibility of a pregnancy. Maybe because it wasn't an option. Maybe because of the birth control pills I'd been taking for years.

I found pleasure and peace in being alone with Bill and in the complex conversations we had about everything. My child-wanting had carved a wariness in him, and a distance between us that came from this one stunning difference in our wants. In the deserts of Utah, far enough away from the hopes of family, my longing stepped back and gave me room to breathe.

Late in the afternoons we took walks up dry washes. I touched my hands on canyon walls powdered with sandstone dust. Layers of time marked in sediment like earthy sunsets: green, white, orange, brown, red, lavender.

Ancient erosion wore away grain of sand by grain of sand, and made formations: arched bridges, elephants, kings with crowns, three women in a row. Always a new shape to be found.

One evening in Bryce, we sat on the rim of the canyon and watched another sunset, the last we would have after our days in the desert. We sat with bent knees, shoulder to shoulder, hip to hip, our hands behind us, flat on the sandy earth. The air cooled as the sun went down.

The sky went brilliant and brilliant and brilliant again. Bill put his arms around me. The desert would become my favorite place. We would come back again and again. I felt different here, free of the wanting. This gave me a clear view of the ways Bill met me. All of him: generous, vulnerable, honest. I wanted this to be enough.

26. LIKE AN UNASKED PRAYER

COLLEGE AND EUGENE WERE strange territories to me. The city, 250 miles west and south of Condon, had stoplights and one-way streets and freeways to navigate, strangers and apartments and rent to pay, people on bicycles, runners in shorts and strappy T-shirts, men with long hair and beards, women who didn't wear makeup or shave their legs. Patchouli oil. Hibachi smoke. Cedar trees and fir trees and ivy and rain.

I felt small town and unsure, excited and curious. There were psychology classes teaching me the ways the mind works, and books that made me reconsider my beliefs about the world. There were boys I didn't know.

In a women's restroom on campus, a few weeks into my first year, I saw a sign for Planned Parenthood: *Low-Cost Birth Control*.

I made a doctor appointment for myself for the first time and sat in the waiting room alone and filled out the forms. In the exam room, the nurse handed me a pale robe and told me to take my clothes off. I raised my feet to metal stirrups, felt the cool of a speculum. The doctor said, "Relax your knees." The pressure of the speculum opening inside me.

The doctor held up a long cotton swab. "This might sting

a little." The swab touched the center of me, harsh and dry. I looked everywhere except at her.

She released the speculum, handed me a tissue, patted my knee. "That's it," she said.

The nurse gave me a plastic cup with my name written on the outside. She told me how to start and stop and start again for a clean catch. I pretended that peeing in a cup was normal.

The packet of birth control pills came with an oval case. Back in my apartment I fit the circle of twenty-one tiny yellow pills and seven white into the case and set it in on the dresser next to my bed.

The nurse had told me to take the first pill on the Sunday after I started my next period. On that morning, I pressed the plastic bubble, pushed the yellow pill through the aluminum backing, held that pill in the palm of my hand, and put it in my mouth.

Each morning I took those pills. And, like an unasked prayer, the acne I'd struggled with since my sophomore year in high school cleared up as the doctor had said it might. I was safe to carry on as I had been, with boys I knew and boys I didn't know.

27. SECRETS AND CALCULATIONS

IN THE FIRST YEARS of my marriage to Bill, I tried to wrangle the baby wanting in me back down. I went on as though nothing had changed. And, from the outside, nothing had.

Each morning, as I'd done since college, I pressed a tiny yellow pill through the tinfoil at the back of its plastic bubble. Cupped my hand to catch it. Bill was asleep or already at work. I was alone in the bathroom.

This was my ritual, what I had done for most of fourteen years, without thinking of what I was saying yes to. Or saying no to. My periods came every fourth Tuesday in the week of the white sugar pills placed in the packet as markers to keep a woman who didn't want children in the habit of taking her daily pill.

But now, on some mornings, I paused. Me, the mirror, these pills.

What if?

If I stopped. If Bill didn't know. If I became pregnant anyway. Would he finally surrender? Or would he push me to end the pregnancy? Would he leave? Would he fall in love with the child?

The me with the pill in her palm caught eyes with the me in the mirror, the woman I would have to face, the child in her arms come to life from secrets and calculation. A child I didn't want that way. A relationship I didn't want that way.

I wouldn't do it. Honesty was what we had, Bill and I, what I valued as much as the way he made me laugh, as much as the way he told me, daily, that he loved me. We were not made of secrets and calculations.

IT WAS AS THOUGH there were two parts of me, two separate women.

The woman of my logic embraced common sense and plans and agreements. She took pleasure in her life. The freedoms, career, friends. The family already here. The exquisite moments. This woman said, *You have enough.*

This woman understood the struggles of mothering, the demands and self-sacrifice, the always being torn between work and child, self and child. This woman took in the love of other people's children and gave it back completely, joyfully. She said, *If you have children of your own, you won't have the time or energy or love for these children already here.*

The woman of my body pushed against logic. The woman of my body leaned to the pull of history and family expectation. Leaned so far that her body yearned. This woman said, *Now. Before it is too late.*

The yearning distilled into a singular desire that overwhelmed logic and common sense. I wanted to be pregnant. To be filled with baby and movement of baby. To have my breasts swell, belly grow, to feel the pressure and weight of carrying within. I wanted to run my hands over the taut skin that sheltered a soon-to-be child and know the pains of a baby pushing out.

Words I'd once heard Mom say echoed in my sleep. *The women in our family have easy pregnancies.* In my sleep my belly grew with a dreamed-up baby. I dreamed the special attention that a pregnant woman gets, the chair given up, the soft eyes and hopeful questions, the baby gifts and baby shower. I dreamed a hurried hospital drive, the birth beginning.

In these dreams I never had the baby.

Waking was a loss. I ran my hands down my flat stomach, over my small breasts. Next to me, Bill slept, his leg long against mine.

Did the dreams mean I was making the wrong choice? Were my dreams my secret truth?

I told Bill, "I dreamed I was pregnant." Or "I was in labor. It didn't hurt." I told him how much I loved it. "This is the part I feel like I'm missing," I said. "I can't know what it's like to have a baby in me. To give birth."

Bill stayed quiet. Because I tried to keep my wanting small, to not burden him, he didn't know how big it was. To him, my dream-telling must have sounded the same as when I told him my dream of driving off a road into a lake and the water was rising; the dream of putting on new running shoes and I could fly; the dreams of the man or boys or killer bees outside the door and me inside terrified.

I said, "The women in my family have easy pregnancies."

Bill did not pick up this hopeful offering.

The dreams of pregnancy and almost-birth held in me through the day. In the skin of me, the blood of me, the womb of me.

28. HIS DREAM CHILD

I FILL IN THE picture: Bill as a boy of eleven stretched out on a sofa, legs going long and lean, magazine folded back on itself. He sits up to look closer at the words in an advertisement. A book: *The Magic of Believing: Get what you want through the power of your belief.*

He saves his nickels and dimes and trades them in for one-dollar bills. He sends them in, orders the book. The beginning of his searching self.

The books he'd read since that first one, his self-exploration, classes he'd taken. What did he want to believe? What was he searching for? In all of that searching, hadn't he ever questioned the absence of his desire for a child?

Finally, in one of my times of pressing for more, he offered a new clue, something I hadn't heard before.

He said, "If anyone had told me when I was a boy that I wouldn't have children of my own, I'd have said they were crazy."

My body leaned into this surprise. Heart-skip beat of possibility. Was there really a time when it had been as natural for Bill to think he would grow up to be a father as it had been for me to think I would be a mother?

The magic was in me now. Maybe this was the clue, the key to the hidden door that would open his mind to the possibility of a child.

"But after I grew up, every time the idea of having a child came up with a woman," Bill said, "my answer was no. A strong no. I didn't want kids."

Oh.

The key drops, the door is solid. Back to where we'd always been.

"Then I took a class on dreams," Bill said. "This was a few years before I met you."

I leaned in again.

"I told the teacher I had a recurring dream. I'd had it for years. In the dream I'm accused of killing someone. Everyone says I did it. They say it so often that I start to think maybe it's true."

The dream leader asked, *Could it be that, in this dream, you are killing your child self?*

Again, the possibility. If he knew the source of his no, maybe he would change his mind. "It made so much sense," Bill said. "I had to grow up way too fast. I didn't get to be a child when I was a child. Having a kid would be giving up myself all over again."

He said this like it was true. That it decided everything. Door locked, barricaded, sealed.

I wanted to push into this dream, to ask, *Isn't it possible you are killing possibility? The hope for a child you might have? Isn't it possible that having a child would make up for what you didn't get from your dad?*

But I am no dream guide.

The meaning in our dreams is only what the dreamer makes of it.

Bill said, "After that workshop, the dream stopped."

Can a man who never got to be a child have a child? Would he know the child's need to play, laugh, shout, be selfish, cry, need, need, need, demand? Could I give him a crash-course, fast-course, learn-it-now-course in childhood so that he could overcome? Does anyone ever overcome? Why should he have to be the one to overcome?

29. THE QUESTION OF MY FUTURE

IN MY SECOND YEAR of college in the fall of 1977, I stopped being with so many boys and settled with someone new.

In one call, I told Mom I was dating a new guy.

In one call, I told Mom he wasn't in college and that he worked at the place where I was doing work-study.

In one call, I told Mom he was older than me.

"How old?"

"Thirty-one."

Silence. White space filled with simple math: I was nineteen.

"That is old."

"I'm moving in with him."

Silence.

"I'll save money."

I didn't say what seemed as true as it had with all the boys before him: *He loves me. I love him.* I didn't know that the first hot breathlessness wasn't love. I couldn't see that I was confusing my loneliness and this man's attention with love.

In Condon, the kids I'd gone to kindergarten with were the same kids I graduated high school with. I'd never learned how to make new friends. I felt shy and different in this college town, and by my second year, my loneliness grew. This man washed away the loneliness.

Years later, Mom would tell me she worried. "I was afraid I'd lose you," she'd say. "I didn't know what to do, but I thought if I tried to stop you, you'd turn away, so far away you might not come back." She'd tell me she always worried about me, through those years of high school and college and my early twenties. Worried I would be the child she'd lose. Not through death, but that I would turn away from family, be drawn into something she couldn't pull me back from, and I'd be gone. "You were always trying new things," she says. "Things I didn't understand. Pushing up against the edges."

But she didn't tell me this during that phone call. I wouldn't have listened anyway.

MAYBE IT'S ONLY POSSIBLE to speak of the hardest times in a family long after they are over. Maybe it's only possible to know how bad it was long after the time has passed.

During that winter, Mom wrote me letters and I went home less. Going home meant feeling the disapproval and tension behind Mom and Dad's unasked questions about this older man.

Mom wrote letters that came empty of the monthly checks she used to send, an emptiness filled with the disapproval she wouldn't speak of.

In her letters she wrote of the terrible winter they were having in Condon. An ice storm on top of snow. Frozen water lines and broken power poles, and a weeklong power outage. Everyone with the flu. Nana was sick and getting tests for what would turn out to be lung cancer. Mom was taking care of Nana, and Dad's drinking had gotten worse. Mom wrote that Dad was no help to her at all.

In those letters Mom never asked about my new living situation or about the man I was with. A man I'd let into my life in the same casual way I'd let all the boys up until then in, without thought about the long term.

Instead of asking about him or my plans, or telling me about the disappointment I knew she had, Mom sent articles by women like Judith Viorst, who wrote about womanhood and aging and grief and love. Mom said how good Viorst was at presenting all sides of things and "makes no cut-and-dried conclusions."

When I read Mom's letters now, I see her words, like tracing paper, barely covering her worry. She was trying to reach me. These letters, the articles, the books she mentioned she was reading, were enough to keep me to her. She saw possibility in me and would hang on until I found it myself.

Even though I fought her quiet disapproval, it leaked into me and into my relationship with my boyfriend, leaving dark trails that drew my attention to our differences. The twelve years between our ages made him not fit with the few friends I had, or me fit with his. Me pushing toward a degree and a career, him happy to get high each night and eat two bowls of chocolate chip mint ice cream in front of the TV.

I stopped wanting him to touch me or look at me with all his love. I couldn't tell if this was me falling out of love or me wanting my parents' love more than his.

Summer.

"I have to go home and work," I said. I had a summer job in Condon, driving truck for a wheat harvest crew.

"When will you be back?" my boyfriend asked.

"I'll be back at the end of summer. We work long days. I won't have time to get away." I didn't know if this was true or not.

All through the summer Mom and Dad and I stepped around the big fat question of my future. The question I knew they had but gave them no opening to ask.

I worked my harvest job, went out with friends, went to parties. Spent time with other boys. My boyfriend called from Eugene every week. Long silences in long-distance calls that held the distance I felt but couldn't explain and didn't want to admit to anyone because it would mean I'd been wrong.

On a Saturday night in August, near the end of harvest season, I was in my bedroom getting ready to go out to a party. Curling iron cooling on the dresser, hair feathered back, eye shadow dark, beaded leather choker around my neck. Mom and Dad came up the stairs and into my room. They'd never done a thing like that before. Both of them together. To "have a talk" with me.

Dad said, "Your mother and I want to know what your plans are this fall." Serious. Formal. Sober.

"I'm going back to Eugene."

"Are you still going to live with him?" Mom said, more to the point. Tense. Sharp voice.

The air they exhaled had a need in it, a need I could almost breathe into myself.

"I don't know." The push and the pull. I didn't want to go back to him. I didn't want to tell them they were right.

"You need to decide." Mom folded her arms. Took a position. "We're not going to send you any money if you're living with him."

"Fine." I set my legs solid. Folded my own arms. "I can take care of myself." I hoped they couldn't hear the shake in my voice.

"How?"

"Summer money. Work-study," I listed on thrust-out fingers, raised-up voice. "I'm paying for school anyway. You already told me I'm the one who has to pay off the loans."

The flinch in Dad, the shake of his head.

Mom made her own list, used her own thrust-out fingers. "There's the gas card you've got, plus the fill-up you do every time you come home. The food we send back with you, your car insurance, your health insurance, your car. All the money we've sent already."

Her voice raised, my voice raised. I started to cry.

"You stopped," I said. "You've hardly sent any."

Dad stepped toward me. "Babe," he said, "we want to know if you're going to keep living with him."

"I don't know. I don't know," I yelled. I grabbed my purse and went out of the bedroom, down the stairs, out the door, and through the front gate to my car. My tires spit gravel as I drove away. I went to a party and stayed out late enough that my staying-up-late-mom would be in bed.

She'd left the lamp on in my room. The light shone on two small pieces of notepaper sitting on the dresser. Mom's big loopy lettering.

I was a little drunk, but the words were clear.

> *All I want is for you to be happy.*
> *A) Make your own decisions.*
> *B) Live your own life.*
> *Just don't shortchange yourself in the process.*
> *I love you and that's what counts—(we only want to*
>   *be proud of you).*
> *Do what you are big enough to do.*
> *Love, Mom*

Maybe it's possible to know a moment when you are changed. To recall that moment for the rest of your life. The shifting, like all my cells moved to a new place. Blood, tissue, heart, stomach, brain. That moment when a girl takes the step from being a teenager to being an adult. To stand in someone else's shoes, see the world from that place, to understand that all Mom was doing (the arguments, the worry, the silences) was for this. For me to be happy.

I kept that note, tucked it away in an envelope.

All I needed to do was figure out how to be happy.

To show her I could be happy.

30. PRECIOUS THINGS

AT FIRST, FROM THE outside, Bill and I must have looked like a newly married couple planning to have children. Anyone could see we were in love. Anyone could see we were making a home together. Anyone could see how much we opened our hearts to other people's children.

We lived in Bill's house, and I put my own touch on it: a new sofa and love seat for the living room, the bedroom furniture that had belonged to my grandparents went into the guest room, Nana's china and Aunt Lena's cut glass in a new teak cabinet. The tall tropical plants that Bill's ex-wife had left behind gradually died, and I replaced them with the hardy plants that kept on no matter what. Lipstick, hoya, mother-in-law's tongue.

Hardly anyone asked about our plans. Maybe they thought it was for children that Bill and I had finally married after three years together. Me still young enough to be fertile. Bill still young enough to not be a terribly old father. Maybe they figured it was a matter of time before we announced some news.

Time went by. One year. Two. Our home began to tell the answers to questions no one asked. I took on the garden, pulled out the big square of lawn and added terraced rock walls and tall grasses. Who would do this if they were going to have children? Children need grass to run in. Who would buy a glass dining table with sharp corners? A white carpet?

These were the luxuries of a childless life. I could have precious things. When we traveled, I could leave those rocks, those tall grasses, and not worry about a lawn overgrowing and turning brown. We could sleep late, make love loud, eat when we wanted.

IN LATE SUMMER, TWO years into our marriage, Bill and I went with a group of friends to the countryside west of Portland to see a piece of property one couple had recently purchased. The land was grassy meadow surrounded by cedars. The new landowners walked through the long grass, bending a path to show where they might build a house overlooking the valley. All the other couples had children, but they'd left them at home. We started to set up a picnic.

The husband of one couple that I didn't know well walked to the car with me when I went to get a blanket and the fruit and cheese I'd prepared. By now our friends knew we traveled, and this man asked about our latest trip to the Olympic National Park. I told him about hiking in the Hoh Rain Forest. The mossy ground that made each step a whisper, the nurse trees, fallen cedars giving life to new saplings.

This man said he'd love to go there. "But, you know"—he glanced back at his wife—"we're pretty busy. The kids. Hard to get away." His wife used to be slim and strong, a runner. She used to wear lipstick. Now she had dark circles under her eyes, a thickened waist, pale lips.

He said, "Are you and Bill going to have kids?"

He and his wife had two kids and, whenever I saw him with them, one or the other leaned up against him, arms wrapped around his legs, his hand stroking downy child hair. I figured he would tell me how great it was, that he loved being a dad, that he'd had no idea how amazing it would be.

"We're not," I said. I took a breath, getting ready to tell him why.

Before I got past that breath, he said, "That's really cool." He lowered his voice. "You guys are living the kind of life I'd like to have. Traveling. Free." He shrugged. "It's hard. You know. I mean don't get me wrong, I love my kids. But. If I had to do it over again." He folded his arms across his chest. Looked down at his feet, white tennis shoes dusty. He was telling me of a secret affair with a life he didn't have. He shrugged. "You miss out on other stuff. You know? So it's cool. That you have the guts to not do what everyone expects."

Up until now I'd known only the romance I made up, of men with pregnant wives. His hand on her belly, feeling the heartbeat. Talking of names. Him taking care of her. The romance of men in the birthing room, his hand gripped by hers as she pushed and he brushed the hair from her forehead, urging her on. The romance of men with their babies. Two big hands holding a tiny infant. A toddler hugging her father's leg, him lifting her up. Big smile on his face, sunshine and daisies in a field.

But here was this man, telling me the value of my choice. Part of me wanted to hug him, for the relief his words gave me. Another part wanted to shake him. For telling me. The secret in it. Had he known this before he had his children? Did she know about his regret? I didn't think so, not with how he kept glancing over his shoulder.

A jolt of love for Bill spread through me. He was a man who told me everything inside him. He drew his lines clearly: *This is what I will do. This is what I will not do.* He did not have regret.

Which man would I choose if I had the choice?

The one I'd already chosen.

But still.

31. RED INK AND SIDE NOTES

BILL'S FATHER WENT FROM marriage to army. He went to faraway Korea. Every year he spent two weeks of leave with his kids. What did this military man who had left his children do with them for two whole weeks?

He took them to his mother's house. He took them to the ocean. He took them to the mountains.

The children hungered for the mystery father. For two whole weeks they fought for his attention. Elbows and whines, tears and score-keeping. Who gets the front seat? Who gets to sit next to him at dinner? Who gets to sleep with him at night?

Sleeping arrangements were on rotation. Every third night Bill got to share the bed with his father. A child fidgets. A father who could leave his children doesn't know a child falling to sleep can't be still.

After too many flops and leg stirs, humming and long breaths, his father says, *If you move one more inch I'm going to make you sleep in the other room with your brother and sister.*

But the itch on his cheek.

"I moved my arm so slow," Bill tells me. I imagine him as boy-child. How slowly can he move his arm? Slow slow slow. So his father doesn't hear the rustling of the covers, the held breath. The desperate need to scratch that itch. Maybe he can't be quiet enough. Maybe he loses his one-third nights with his father. And that is it for the rest of the year.

BILL WRITES A LETTER like he's learning to write letters in school. Seven years old and the letter goes like this:

Dear Dad How are you I am fine the weather here is nice.

And so on.

"I addressed it," Bill tells me. "Mom took me to the post office for stamps. I put the stamps on and put it in the letter slot."

This boy in worn pants and worn shoes goes every day to the mailbox next to the road. "I waited for weeks. Maybe a month." Not realizing how long it takes a letter to get to Korea. For another letter to come back from Korea.

And one day a letter is there.

He carries it into the house, balanced on the palms of hands, to the bedroom where he can be alone with his father's letter addressed just to him. He opens the envelope, unfolds the pages. Here is the letter he wrote to his father. Marked up in red ink. Red question mark where the question mark should have been. Crossed out misspelled words. A note: *You need to try harder in school.*

Maybe there's also a letter with Bill's marked up letter. Maybe his Dad says something else. What Bill remembers is the red ink, the disappointment.

"I'M A TERRIBLE WRITER," Bill said. "I really struggled in school with spelling and punctuation."

At first, I didn't believe him. At first, I thought he was joking when he asked me how to spell words that seemed simple to me.

Towel. Sure. Pleasant.

How could this man, so smart about a thousand things, not be able to spell common words?

At first I said, "Sound it out," in a know-it-all voice, which maybe sounded like his father.

Until I saw his face. Until I searched for the clues. Until he told me the story of writing to his dad.

I drew lines between that father and the man I loved.

My search to know why Bill didn't want a child led me to know him.

AT NIGHT I WOULD get into bed and turn and toss and plump my pillow two, three, five times. Making my sleeping nest. Pillow just right. Blankets just right. Bangs out of eyes. Pillow again. The tension of Bill next to me. "What are you doing? Could you be still?"

His harsh tone.

Me, quiet, trying not to move.

Him saying, "I'm sorry."

Him saying, "You would think of all people I wouldn't do that."

Knowing where your scars come from doesn't make them go away.

32. ON THE WAY TO A GROWN-UP LIFE

WHEN I LEFT MY summer job in Condon to go back to college for my junior year, I didn't know I would never live in my parents' home again.

I broke things off with the older man, got my own apartment, and focused on my studies. But I still wanted love. The kind that lasted. And, while I thought it was possible to have the always-excited never-ending love, I tried to be more like Leanne, to have a plan for who might be the right person for the long term.

It didn't take me long to find someone who I thought would fit well into my future and into my parents' wishes for me.

At a college party, I felt a tap on my shoulder. "Jackie Shannon?" This new man was slim and muscular with hair feathered and styled.

I recognized him. Sam. He'd lived in Condon until he was thirteen. He'd been a friend of Brad's, and his parents had been friends of my parents. Back then he had short hair and thick-rimmed glasses. He and his family had moved away when I was eleven, and I hadn't seen him since.

We went outside and stood in the driveway while kids in

vests and flare-legged pants went in and out of the party house. We talked about my family and his, people we knew from Condon. He was almost finished with his degree at the university. He was way cuter than I remembered.

He asked me what I liked to read.

"Oh, you know," I said. I thought of the books I read when I got bored of textbooks. Sidney Sheldon, Jackie Collins, romance novels. I shrugged. "I'm drawing a blank right now."

He said he'd turn me on to some new stuff, good books.

Within days I'd fallen into bed with him. Within days I was falling in love again.

THAT FALL WAS COLDER than usual for Eugene. The heat in my apartment was unpredictable. Sam's apartment was warm and had books and a stereo and a long comfortable sofa.

He gave me a book of short stories by Raymond Carver: *Will You Please Be Quiet, Please?* The world of reading and books changed for me then; stories could be simple and real and about the kind of people I grew up with.

Sam remembered overnights at our place when he was a boy, how cool it was to go out to the barn and ride the horses and hang out in the bunkhouse. He knew about the bunkhouse and the barn and the horses. He knew Condon and my family.

The familiarity of him was a relief, but he was enough different. He'd been to Europe! He knew about literature and poetry! He danced with me, the two of us alone in his apartment!

Within a few months I took him to Condon, the same weekend Nana went into the hospital in Portland with her lungs full of fluid. After that weekend Mom sent a letter.

> *Just a little note to say we enjoyed the weekend. Everyone liked Sam—of course it was easier since we had known him as a boy. He is on the top of Crisi's list. He really drew her out and talked to her like an adult. . . .*

This path would make her happy. This path seemed right, the way fairy tales ended, happily ever after. We couldn't know more worry would come. Things I had control over and things I didn't.

Mom's letter said this too:

> *I'm glad you stopped to see Nana. I talked to the doctor, and I'm afraid the tumor is malignant. . . .*

On that visit to Nana in the hospital in Portland, Sam had held my hand down the long hall to her room. She sat up and raised her arms to hug me when we came in. She was tiny and pale against the white of the sheets and pillow. "Oh, there's my college girl." She remembered Sam and asked about his family. We only stayed a while. When we left, I stopped outside her room. I began to cry. I'd never been around a dying person, but I knew that was what was happening. Sam put his arms around me. For the first time, I felt the comfort of letting a man hold me in my sadness, hold me for some other reason than love or sex.

AFTER CHRISTMAS I MOVED in with Sam. No one said how it was like the year before, a pattern, me moving in with a man for the second year in a row. But this time there was no icy disapproval. Sam was from home. He was only a few years older than me. I was happy. This time my family was happy too.

Early spring, slow dancing to Chicago's "Happy Man," both of us easy on bourbon, Sam asked me to marry him. I said yes. Mom was eighteen when she married. Leanne was nineteen, and so was Pat. Some of my friends had already married. We would wait until the following spring. I would be twenty-one by then. Grown-up. An age of sureness.

I called home and told Mom and Dad the news, and also that I wouldn't be coming home at the end of the school year. I would take classes through the summer and graduate early the following spring. The wedding would be in Condon right after. Then I would start work and begin paying back my college loans.

Leanne sent me a letter of congratulations on our engagement. She said she thought Mom and Dad might be a little sad that I wasn't coming home again, except to visit. She said,

> *We have all thought of you as a college student for so long, it's hard to change one's long-range thinking, but by next spring I'm sure everyone will have adjusted to the idea of you being a career girl. Anyway, I wish you the best in your marriage and your career.*

And she said this,

> *I don't know how much Mom and Dad have told you, but Nana isn't very well and if you want to see her, you should come home soon.*

I went to Condon for one last visit with Nana.

33. FAULT LINE

IN 1993, BILL AND I had been married for three years when my friend Amy called. Ten years earlier, Amy and had I met in classes we were taking in Eugene. Classes of self-exploration and personal growth that formed a tight bond between the people who attended. We immediately connected and sustained that connection. Now, even though Amy still lived in Eugene and I'd moved to Portland, we got together regularly.

I considered her my best friend. Over the years, we'd shared the excitement of job successes and the sweet moments of falling in love. And we'd comforted each other through the hard endings of relationships.

This was the terrain under us. I'd seen her at her best and her worst. I thought she'd seen me at mine.

"Guess what, Jack?" she said.

I knew what she'd say. I knew she and her husband were trying.

"I'm pregnant," she said.

Her words should have been almost as exciting for me as they were for her. I *was* excited. I would be the best friend of this baby's mom. But next to that excitement I felt like I'd lost a race I hadn't known I'd put myself in.

I'd met Bill before Amy met her husband. She'd looked at

the relationship Bill and I were building, and she wanted one like it. Maybe I'd felt proud that I'd found someone like Bill first while she still aspired to the kind of love I had. Then she met her husband and we were even. Now Amy had a baby in her belly, and her husband wanted the baby as much as she did.

AMY CAME TO VISIT in her seventh month, a last chance for us to be together before everything changed. Bill was gone for the weekend. He wouldn't see how beautiful Amy was in her leggings and the body-hugging top that showed her pregnant belly. Pregnant women now no longer wore the loose maternity blouses and dresses our mothers had worn, silly and frilly and hiding. They dressed like this, like Amy. Stretchy clothes that said: *look here, look at what I carry, look at what I am creating.*

That Saturday, we did the things we always did when we were together: Chinese food, bookstores, a movie, talk, hook arms and walk down the street, her long dark wavy hair, my long dark straight hair, my strong lean body, her beautiful pregnant body. People passed us, hopeful smiles to her belly. Women asked when she was due, asked if she hoped for a boy or a girl. All eyes on Amy and her belly.

I couldn't keep my eyes off her either, the same way I couldn't keep my eyes off a pregnant woman at a party or in a store, the woman in Accounting coming to me in my new job in Human Resources to fill out the paperwork for her three months of maternity leave.

I wanted three months' leave from work. I wanted the looks, the baby shower, the seat given up to let me have a rest with what I carried. I wanted that belly. Her hand went to it, without even thinking. What was it? A twinge, a pain, maybe simply holding up the weight. What was she touching, her own skin or the life beneath it? The flutter of movement within, a comforting pat to that child she maybe already knew more intimately than anything could be known.

I didn't ask. I didn't tell her about the wondering-what-if-maybe part of me.

Amy stopped with chopsticks above her plate, long thin fingers. "It's amazing, Jack," she said. "To have this life in me." Her husband probably put his mouth to her belly, whispered to their child.

"Feel it," she said, next to me at the bookstore. She took my hand and put it on her belly. The look on her face, like she had the best secret, right there inside her. She knew what it was like to have the bleeding stop, to see the blue line on the tester, to feel her belly-skin stretch, first swirl of movement, a tiny handprint, pressed from inside.

Her baby wasn't the first child I'd felt kick. It wouldn't be the last. I smiled. I said, "That is really cool. Wow. Amazing." I was happy for her and this was all I would show. If I said I wasn't sure, if I said I was jealous, if I said I wished, then it would take away from what she had. Saying these truths would take away from what I had, and from the bright shiny confident way I wanted to look to the world.

LATE IN THE EVENING, Amy said, "I still have your aunt Lena's rocking chair. I'd like to keep it for the baby."

The rocking chair I'd brought from Condon to Eugene not long after Sam and I married. My great aunt Lena had died, and Mom and Dad let us kids have some of her furniture. I'd picked a mirrored china cabinet, an oak desk, and that chair. Leanne had wanted the rocking chair for the babies she already had. But when it was my turn to choose, I took it.

Back then I'd thought Sam and I would have a child to rock in that chair. But things changed. When I moved from Eugene to Portland, I didn't have room for the rocking chair or the other furniture I'd gotten from Aunt Lena. I left it behind for Amy to store. I couldn't take it from her now, another mother wanting to rock her child.

EARLY ON SUNDAY MORNING, the metal blinds in my bedroom knocked against the windowsill quick and loud. Everything shook. I ran out into the living room. The shaking, the noise, the long fault line we'd been warned about. A vase shivered across a shelf and fell. A sound, a roaring, outside.

Then it all stopped. Only a few long seconds had gone by.

"Jack?" Amy came out of her room, her dark eyes gone darker. "What was that?" She held her belly. One hand on top, one hand under. Afraid for more than herself.

"Earthquake," I said. "That was really cool, huh?" I sounded smug in my this-is-no-big-deal voice.

We looked at the vase, unbroken on the carpet. Waited for the ground to move again. Her life wasn't only hers anymore.

AFTER AMY'S BABY WAS born, Bill and I drove south to Eugene for the weekend. We went to Amy's house. I gave her a gift for her boy. I don't remember what that gift was, but I remember the way Amy looked at her baby when she took us to his bedroom. He was asleep. She leaned over the crib and stared at him with a private smile. As though Bill and I weren't there with her.

Bill looked at the baby and put his arm around Amy and said, "I'm happy for you." And he stepped back and made room for me. I bent over the crib for a long time looking at her boy. His head was bald, except for some blond fuzz. His mouth moved in tiny sleep moves.

"I'm sorry you can't hold him," Amy said. "But I don't want him to wake up." I didn't mind not getting to hold him. This surprised me.

She stood beside me and we watched him. "I had no idea it would be like this," she said. "It's like nothing I've ever felt. You can't imagine. I sometimes put him next to me on the bed and I stretch out with him and the whole afternoon goes by just watching him. I love him so much."

I'd always been interested in new-mother stories. But now I felt bored. This surprised me too.

Looking back, I must have had some sense of loss. The old ways of our friendship gone. This baby was now the center of things. But I went past that fast. It was too late; the baby was here.

Aunt Lena's rocking chair was in the corner, the dark old wood. I stepped over and touched the arm of it. Aunt Lena never rocked a baby in this chair. Amy had this bedroom with this baby and this rocking chair. I loved my friend for her happiness and I resented her for telling me she had what I couldn't know.

I looked over at Bill. He was looking out the window at the yard below.

We didn't stay long. The baby was sleeping, and there didn't seem to be much else to talk about. Besides, we were staying with other friends, friends who didn't have a child and who could go out to dinner with us and stay up late and not worry about a schedule and feeding and quiet.

THE NEXT TIME I saw Amy, her baby was six months old. It would be the last time I saw her until her boy became a man.

She came to Portland with her husband. They didn't stay with us. She asked me to come to her at the Heathman Hotel. "It's easier," she said. "All the stuff it takes to go anywhere with a baby."

Never mind that I was working more than full-time, that I would have to drive downtown in traffic, take time out of my busy workday. "Oh, no problem," I said. "I'll come to you."

After I hung up, I told Bill how it bothered me. Ever since she'd met her husband, she hardly spent time with me. Having a baby meant everyone had to work around it. I took my stand, counting the reasons to step away from her.

I spent extra time getting dressed that day. Heels, a slim skirt, a silk blouse, a bright scarf. I was the professional, the working woman. She was the mother with a baby.

In the hotel room, I held her boy on my lap. I touched his downy hair. His perfect round head. Already he was smiling, catching eyes, taking my hand and pulling himself up. Amy took a picture of her boy and me. My profile looking at him, smiling. His profile looking at me, smiling. My long hair, that bright scarf.

I didn't hold him for long: he got fussy. I didn't stay long:

he needed a nap. When we said goodbye, we said we'd see each other again soon.

Later Amy sent a copy of that picture. Me and her boy. I pinned it to my wall of pictures of nieces and nephews and friends' kids, pictures of Bill and me in front of pyramids and sandstone and mountains. Bill and me holding kids and playing with kids. I looked beautiful and happy with that big baby boy in my lap. In that picture, there is no hint of the longing in me.

LATER, THE FINAL SHIFTING, settling. Something Amy said or didn't say, an effort she didn't make. The relief I felt that I already had plans when she tried to visit and she was busy when I tried.

She felt the shifting, the distance growing. She tried to find out why, to fix it. I gave her small reasons, reasons that didn't make sense. About her not coming to see us, about her husband seeming not interested in us, about me having to come to her rather than her to me. In her last long letter, she said the loss of our friendship devastated her. She didn't understand. She hurt. She said she would stop trying to reach out. She said, "The ball is in your court."

I didn't pick it up.

34. THINGS THAT COME IN THREES

THE FIRST OF THE things that came in threes happened on May 4, 1979. Good news. Pat's second child, John Dale, who would be called JD, was born. A grandson for my parents. Dad was of a different generation and this boy was a legacy.

The second of the three was news we knew was coming. Nana died on May 8, and Sam and I went home to Condon for her funeral. Saw her one last time in her casket at the mortuary. I didn't yet know all the questions I hadn't asked her about her life. Or that death entered like this. You knew it was coming and you should make yourself as ready as possible to meet it. You were never ready.

The third thing of three was the unlucky, the random, the thing that isn't supposed to happen to a girl finding her way to the life she thinks will make her happy. It isn't supposed to happen to any girl.

Sam worked at a convenience store through the nights while I studied and slept. In the early morning of May 19, I was asleep. And then awake to a whisper shout in the bedroom.

—Wake up. Shut up.

A tall silhouette in dawn light. A man. A mask. Butcher knife in hand.

—Do what I say or I'll kill you.

Always I'd thought that if a man did what this man was here to do, I would fight. I would run. This is not what I did. This is not what my body did.

I did what he said.

—Get out of bed. Crawl. Lie face down on the carpet.

Fear-breath breathes shag and dust and the footsteps of others.

Fear-breath makes noise. Loud to me. Loud to him.

—Shut up or I'll shove this into you.

Blade of knife against my skin. Towels torn for blindfold and binding and gag. Eyes, wrists, ankles, mouth.

My body trembled, like from winter-cold air. But it was spring. I curled my shoulders in as if this would make it stop.

—Where's your money? Car keys? The cops are looking for me.

Take my money, take the keys, take anything. Words, starved of air, speak fear and the high sound of pleading.

He did not go.

He didn't want money or keys or running from cops.

Over the next two hours, he went back and forth between the day-to-day things of my life: my cupboards and refrigerator, my leftover chicken and bag of chips, my blue backpack and books on statistics and group process, my closet and dresser drawers; and me: my mouth, my breasts, my vagina.

Body numb, mind blank with fear-static, eyes covered. My ears all that were left. Cat ears, tuned to his every move.

In the final moments, his body covered mine. One last time. Knife against ribs. His mouth against my ear.

—You saw me. I'll kill you if you saw me.

No, I said.

I was only twenty years old, but now I knew: *This is how easy it is to die.*

I'm cold, I said.

He moved off me. Loosened my binds. Covered me with a blanket.

Thank you, I said.

The shame of gratitude.

—Don't move for half an hour.

Spring air. Silence.

The farm girl in me knows how to track time.

I look. The front door is open. The sky is blue. The phone cord cut. Run now. Out into that blue morning. To the neighbor for help. To call the police. To talk with Sam. To the questions and hospital and reports, and what next. What next?

35. STAND UP AND CARRY ON

THE NEXT DAY WAS a Sunday, and I always called home on Sunday. I dialed the numbers, listened to the ringing, waited for Mom to answer.

"Hello?" she said, like she always did.

"Mom, it's me, Jackie." Like I always did.

My voice echoed how I felt inside. Still. Stunned. Quiet.

How does a daughter tell her mother?

"A man broke in. I was raped."

How does a mother take this in?

"Oh no." Her harsh breath takes it in.

"I'm okay. I'm not hurt."

What she needed to hear. What I needed to believe. The truth, as far as I could tell then. I had no cuts or bruises, I was still me.

Then, her worries. Closer to home.

"This is going to be hard for your father," she said.

Yes. What else was there to do but understand?

Mom was tired from taking care of Nana through her death, tired from Dad's drinking, his grief a reason for more. Worried that what I was telling her would be another reason.

She offered to come be with me.

No, I'd be okay.

Her coming would mean I wasn't.

And what could anyone do? It had happened. Now we all had to go on.

She didn't need to come. I'd be okay.

IN THE WEEK AFTER the rape I cleaned our apartment of the dark gray fingerprint dust the police had left and the threads from the torn towels the rapist had left. Cleaned to remove all traces of him and of my own fear.

This cleanse was a burying of what had come to me in those hours: *death is here, at any turn.* This knowing held the power to stop me. I didn't want to be stopped. I didn't want to be changed by him in any way.

In the burying, I became a woman with a home that sparkles. Vacuum and dust, scrub baseboards and floors and toilets and sinks, line up cans in cupboard by size, hang clothes by color and style, each turned in the right direction.

Change came anyway.

I walked at night, back and forth to campus. Forced myself to take long strides and not look over my shoulder. Stayed alone at home when Sam worked. Friends asked, was I afraid? I shrugged. I'd formed this one clear rule: I wouldn't be his victim beyond the two hours he'd already taken.

My parents didn't come to me. Mom didn't come. And I honed my skill of understanding why something can't be given, so it doesn't hurt to not receive.

My emotions rose in ambush moments of crying and shaking. Wherever I was, if anyone was there, I left. I was afraid of falling so far apart that I couldn't be gathered again. I didn't want others worrying about me. Their concern was too much to be responsible for. I breathed and swallowed, and got myself under control.

The armor already on me, even before the rape, hardened. I

wanted to look like a girl who could not be hurt, a woman who knew exactly what she was doing.

But fear is sneaky. The knowing trembles underground. It seeps in through cracks and vents, closed eyes and sudden sounds.

Nightmares came to the deep of my sleep. I was alone in a house and someone or something was trying to get in. In my dreams, a scream caught in my throat and I couldn't scream it. I couldn't run.

My nightmares also had the power to wake me. At the exact moment when I couldn't keep the invaders out, the moment when I might die, I woke to the same snared-rabbit fear I'd had that early morning when the rapist came. And I was alive.

I began to lift weights. My arms grew to muscle. I began to run. A block or two at first, more each day, two miles, three, four. My legs grew to muscle. My body armored like topsoil, dampened and then dried, hardening over the buried seed.

Sam and I talked about the case, the facts, the search for the rapist. We didn't speak about how I was. How he was. How what happened might change us. I didn't want to be changed. My plans were the same. To graduate and begin my career in social work. To marry. To have a family. To stand up and carry on as if it hadn't happened at all.

36. LIGHT IN THE CHAPEL

THE SALES GIRL AT the dress store in the mall pulled a plastic bag over the lacy ankle-length dress. "There," she said, tying the plastic at the bottom. "That should keep the rain off it." We both looked out at the March drizzle. It was 1980, ten months after the rape, one month before I would become a wife. The salesgirl didn't know that the ivory-colored dress with its peasant-cap sleeves and empire waist was for my wedding.

I'd told Mom, "I'll buy my dress." I went alone to this store. This is what I needed in those days after the rape. Simple. No complications.

It wasn't really a wedding dress at all.

Mom did most of the preparation: making the cake and the silk-flower bouquets, paying for the bridesmaids' dresses, arranging the reception. In this way, she took care of me, and we had something to talk about because we couldn't speak of the terrible things.

AT MY BRIDAL SHOWER a few weeks before the wedding, the tables were decorated with my chosen colors: peach and gray. I sat at the head table, Mom and my sister-in-law on one side of me, Leanne and Cris on the other. Cris kept track of the ribbons, and Leanne made a list of gifts.

Leanne's first baby was due a few weeks after the wedding. *First comes love, then comes marriage, soon comes Leanne with a baby carriage.*

This was the straight and certain path of her plans. She didn't make a big deal out of being pregnant. I don't remember her even talking about it that much. But then, maybe I never asked.

Big things were happening in the world too: the Iran hostage crisis, the crash of an airliner in Chicago with 273 dead. A Unabomber and IRA bombs and armed robberies. More would happen. In a few months, exactly a year after the rape, Mount St. Helens would explode. The ash covering Oregon would be pushed away by snowplows, and fifty-seven dead would be mourned.

I hardly noticed any of it. My vision had tunneled. The mind, the body, helping me avoid knowing any more than I already knew of the exciting, the sudden, the different, the deadly.

I kept my head down and followed the only plans I had, as though trying to find my way in my sister's footsteps.

Here was love. Here came marriage.

The women of Condon watched as I opened gifts wrapped in silver-and-white paper, mostly careful not to break the ribbon. That tradition of counting possible future children. It felt real and not real. I was there and not there. Bold and insecure, happy and sad.

This box held the Pfaltzgraff stoneware I'd registered for. Mixing bowls, towels, utensils. A dish made of cut glass from Aunt Lena.

I admired each item in an honoring of the giver. At the end of the unwrapping, I stood and thanked the women and told them of the wedding plans. They smiled back at me with their done hair and powdered faces, their love for this girl of their town.

There was no empty chair saved where Nana would have sat, smiling proudly at her college graduate girl about to get married. Death happens in a moment, and the space you took becomes invisible. Only memory holds you here.

At the end of the speech I thanked the hostesses, who were friends of Mom's and the mothers of my friends. The women around the table clapped. This was standing up, this was carrying on.

BACK IN CONDON A month later, on the day before the wedding, Mom and Leanne and Cris gathered around me in my old bedroom. I tried on the lacy dress for them.

"I love it," Leanne said. "But what're you going to wear on your head? You need something."

"I don't want anything fancy." In that year, anything complicated overwhelmed me. Finding the dress, writing the thank-you notes for all those bridal shower gifts, this was all I could do.

Leanne's voice, so like my own. "Jackie," she said, "it's your wedding. You should look like a bride!" She looked like a soon-to-be mother.

Mom snapped her fingers. "I know what you can wear." She opened the closet door and pulled out a box. "This could be your 'something old' and 'something borrowed.'" She held out the half-moon Juliet cap she wore when she married Dad.

Something of hers, something simple. I took it and put it on.

The cap had turned with time to an ivory that matched my dress.

"It's perfect," Mom said.

Leanne looked at me in the mirror. "You should wear some lipstick." She handed me a tube from her purse.

I put it on and stepped back to see the length of me in the mirror. I looked like a bride.

"Pretty," Cris said.

Mom's reflection behind me in the mirror. She moved the cap a little more forward on my head. Her smile. It would be years before I knew the hidden ways she watched over me after I was raped. Worried about how much I exercised. How rigid I became about what I ate. Looked for what might be lurking under my insistent way of moving forward.

•

ON MY WEDDING DAY at the United Church of Christ, Dad and I stood next to each other at the entrance to the chapel. I held the fan bouquet of silk flowers Mom had made. I took his arm and leaned in to his smell of Old Spice and alcohol. He swayed. His lids drooped at half-mast, what my mother used to say to describe his drunken eyes.

We both looked straight ahead at my four-year-old niece Tawna doing her flower-girl walk down the aisle. The light in the chapel was a powdery gold from the frosted windows that went the length of the church.

"Are you ready for this?" Dad said.

The organist pumped the wedding march. I tugged Dad's arm. "Yes," I said. "We should go."

Here comes the bride.

The people of Condon, our families, my few friends from Eugene, the minister, my sisters and sister-in-law in matching bridesmaid dresses, the groomsmen, and Sam looked toward us, me on Dad's arm.

Sam watched me come to him. His smile was full of his love.

Behind him, behind the altar, a stained-glass Jesus filled the whole wall, bigger than life. Vivid reds and blues, a staff in one arm and a lamb in the other. That Jesus had been here through childhood Sundays spent in this church with my mother and brothers and sisters, before each of us, in turn, had gotten old enough to refuse.

At the altar, I let go of Dad and stood next to Sam. With a last look at Jesus, I felt the old ache of longing I used to have when I wished it were me holding that lamb. The tiny circles of wool. The weight of it in the curve of my arm.

OUR RECEPTION AT THE Elks Lodge was like going to another place of worship: my father's place. Low ceilings and dark corners, a room full of people with drinks and cigarettes in hand. It seemed as if all of Condon had come to celebrate my marriage. On one side of the room gifts were piled on a long table next to the wedding cake Mom had decorated with peach-colored roses and silver-foil leaves.

Next to me, Leanne smiled for a picture. When I look at the picture now, I can hardly tell she was only a few weeks away from giving birth. Some small women carry their first child so close and easy you can see why they gladly go on to a second. She was lean with a small mound of belly in the empire-waist dress. She looks happy. Even that far pregnant, she looks happier than me, the bride.

She talked between snaps of the camera. "You know Mom will treat you differently now that you're married."

I held my smile for another flash of bulb and talked out the corner of my mouth. "Really? How?"

"I don't know. Like you're a grown-up, I guess."

That's what I hoped for. To start my grown-up life.

37. ROOTS TOOK HOLD AND RAN THE LENGTH OF MY BODY

IN 1981, SAM AND I rented a townhouse at the west end of Eugene, away from campus. Away from the memory of the rape and all that came after: the victims' panels organized by the police to help survivors recall details that might help them catch our rapist, away from the place of his crime and of his eventual capture near our apartment a year after the rape.

Away from this: Victim.

Toward this: Grown-up. Wife. Career woman.

Our new home had two stories and a back patio with a small patch of dirt. I made my first garden: marigolds in clay pots arranged on wooden shelves on our patio. I put the Pfaltzgraff dishes and mixing bowls in the cupboard, Aunt Lena's cut glass on display on a shelf.

After Granddad died, Mom and Dad had offered some of my grandparents' belongings to us kids. I chose Nana's china with its delicate rouge-colored flowers. Place settings for twelve. I also got their bedroom set. Sam and I carefully arranged the bed with its mahogany headboard and footboard, dressers with brass pulls. It made our bedroom look like the bedroom of two people serious about a long life together.

I was a wife. Each week I made a menu of dinners and a grocery list, and Sam and I went together for groceries. I clipped coupons, cooked the dinners, cleaned the house, did the laundry.

I was a career woman. I worked full-time with clients in an alcohol-treatment program, kept to-do lists and detailed records, and did what I said I would do. My boss liked me. Coworkers liked me. My boss promoted me to supervisor.

I was a future mother. When Aunt Lena died six months after my wedding, she had no children to sort through her precious things. Dad, her favored nephew, was left in charge, and we kids got to choose. I chose the wooden rocking chair, chose it even though Leanne was the one with a baby. I put it in the living room, but I rarely sat in it. It creaked when it rocked, and wasn't so comfortable.

LEANNE'S FIRST PREGNANCY HAD happened during the year after the rape. I'd felt a distance from her joy in the same way I'd felt a distance from my own wedding plans, from Nana's absence in our lives, from Aunt Lena's illness, from the happenings in the world.

Even after Leanne's baby girl was born, I didn't go rushing home. When I did meet my new niece, Annilee, I held her and did the usual cooing that people do over a baby. She was a pretty mix of her dad's dark hair and the shape of his eyes that turned to my sister's eyes when she opened them. All that blue. She was a fine baby, but I didn't mind when Mom or my sister-in-law or someone else nudged in to hold her.

One weekend when Annilee was about ten months old, I went back to Condon for a visit. I spent all Saturday afternoon at Leanne's house. Sam hadn't come with me, and Leanne's husband worked all day, so Leanne and I were alone with Annilee. Already Leanne seemed comfortable being a mom, like she'd been doing it for years. I sat at the kitchen table and Annilee crawled to her and pulled at Leanne's jeans. Leanne bent down to pick Annilee up. Leanne talked to her in a voice I'd never heard her use on anyone else. A voice that sounded like love-no-matter-what, completely there for her girl.

Leanne asked me to watch Annilee while she prepared lunch. Annilee crawled around on hands and knees and pulled herself up, and took a few hanging-on-to-things steps. She stopped at every little thing. She made her way around the edges of the room, pausing here at the spindle-back chair. She touched an envelope with a plastic window that crinkled when she pressed it. She looked at her hand and looked at me, then mashed her fingers a bunch of times on that envelope.

She dropped down and got on her hands and knees and crawled again. Stopped at a corner and sat back on the paddy diaper of her butt, legs crossed. Leaned way forward with one finger out. Reaching. She chased a floaty dust mote with her finger. Caught it. She raised her hand and looked at the dark speck on the tip of her finger. She laughed. She looked at me. Holding that tip of finger up to me.

Here! A dust mote!

For me. From this girl.

My chest expanded with love, as though my heart had grown three sizes and no longer fit. It sent out roots that took hold and ran the length of my body. I wanted to be with her all the time. And if I couldn't do that, I wanted Sam and me to start a child of our own so I could feel this feeling all the time.

SOMETIMES I CRIED AND asked Sam to hold me. He held me. He asked what was wrong.

I was at a distance, out of my body, watching the crying me, held in Sam's lap. "I don't know."

The feeling had no pure identity. It was empty. It was full. It was sadness. It was hope.

I didn't think it was from the rape. I didn't want it to be.

That would be giving the rapist a power I didn't want him to have. And it seemed too easy, too ready a hook to hang my tangled feelings on.

Mostly it felt of time passing, and of a longing for something more.

SOMETIMES WHEN THE TEARS came, Sam pressed me for the reason. I searched. Found words that seemed maybe true. "I'm in this generation. Raised to think we should have it all. Work, marriage, family. It feels like pressure, that I should want it all."

It was 1981. Anything was possible.

I didn't want it all. The love I had felt that day when I watched Annilee was the strongest thing I'd felt for almost two years. And now Leanne was pregnant with her second daughter. She stayed at home and was a mom. I wanted this too.

I felt embarrassed. After all that work going to college. It was important to Mom; she and Dad were proud of me. I couldn't waste it. I was the career woman.

What I said was, "I want to have a baby."

Sam wanted a baby too. I'd seen him with Tawna and JD and Annilee. I'd seen him with his sister's girls. He'd be a good father.

"But how will we afford it?" I said. I worked full-time, Sam worked part-time and was going to graduate school. I made the most money, and my job paid for our health insurance. "I'll have to be home to take care of the baby."

Sam said he'd keep working part-time. He would take care of the baby.

No.

But I didn't say this out loud. Didn't say, *That's not how it's supposed to work. I want to be the mother with her child. I want to stay at home.* The selfishness of it. The old-fashionedness of it.

Sam said we'd figure it out, somehow it would work out.

I didn't know how. I could only hope that when I got pregnant, when the baby came, something would change.

I put the circle of birth control pills away. Quit smoking

and hardly ever drank. To have a baby meant making a healthy body for it. I planned for when.

We began to make love more often, me reaching for Sam. But the rapist had left himself with me. In small ways I stepped outside myself when we made love, so far that I didn't even know it, until years later when another man, another husband, would help me find my way back.

For now, with Sam, each time we made love, the possibility of something new hovered nearby.

38. OTHER PEOPLE'S CHILDREN

MAYBE THE MISSING IN me sent off a scent or a signal. Our friends, and Bill's siblings and mine, were generous with their kids. They always made it happen if I suggested a visit or an outing. Or maybe they were grateful for any small break from the constant demand of being a parent.

By the early nineties, with the birth of Cris's second girl, Devin, Bill and I had thirteen nieces and nephews between us. Even though I'd turned away from Amy and her boy, I got plenty of baby holding and child playing. Most of our friends had kids. Bill and I were full-force fun with them, giving them the special treatment that two people with no children of their own can give.

"The kids love you guys," the parents said. "You're naturals. You should have your own."

"Yeah," I said. "We love kids." I laughed off their words, negated the mothering way in me. What we did for a few hours or a weekend, these parents did for their whole lives. It seemed false to claim that I could be good at something I didn't know.

LEANNE WAS ESPECIALLY GENEROUS in sharing Annilee and Shannon with me. She called whenever an event would bring her and the girls near Portland. She invited me to spend time with her family in Condon and always said yes when, every four or five months, I asked to have the girls for a weekend.

On those weekends I met them in Hood River, midway between Condon and Portland. In the McDonald's parking lot, Leanne hugged her girls goodbye while I put their bags in the trunk. "Have fun," she said. "Be good."

We got in the car. Leanne stood in the parking lot and watched us drive away. "Roll down your windows," I said to the girls. "Wave goodbye to your mom." We waved at Leanne. She was there, waving back.

For all the time I'd spent planning and picking dates and talking with Bill about my excitement, I hadn't thought about what it meant for a mother to send her children off to the city with me. On that first weekend, the girls were just five and seven years old. When I lost sight of Leanne in the rearview mirror, it hit me. She was trusting me with them.

At the stop sign, I looked both ways, once, twice, three times, before proceeding onto the road.

On the freeway, I asked the girls questions about what they wanted to do, told them the plans Bill and I had for the weekend. Spaghetti tonight and Fuddruckers tomorrow, games and putt-putt golf and whatever else they wanted.

With every mile I talked faster, my palms dampened against the steering wheel, and my breath went high up in my chest. We were in this tin can of a car, trucks speeding by, the deep Columbia next to us, and we were going to the city where there were strangers.

I drove slower than normal. Looked in the rearview mirror, side view, ahead, rearview, side view, ahead.

Their lives were in my hands.

Throughout the weekend, I stayed close with my arms out if they ran too fast or climbed too high, wanting them to have the fun of running fast and climbing high but ready for any slip or tumble. I looked both ways crossing streets, once, twice, three times, and held hands tight. At night, I woke, once, twice, three times. I went to the guest room, smoothed their covers, and watched them breathe.

I made a promise to myself. I would protect them always. These girls and all the children in my life. I wouldn't let anything go wrong, whether they were with me or not. If I wouldn't have children of my own, I would do whatever I could to keep the children of my family and of my friends safe.

WHEN THE GIRLS WERE with us, we became a temporary family. At a grocery store, the cashier asked the girls if their mother (me!) would let them have a treat. I held the joy of his mistake for a moment. But before they could answer, I said, "Oh, these are my nieces." Because the girls might think it strange if I pretended they were mine.

"Well, they look like you," the cashier said.

Dark hair, dark hair, dark hair.

Their blue eyes.

My dark eyes.

These girls were not mine.

Even so, when we sat on the couch and Annilee leaned up against me, when Shannon held my hand, I wanted it to be true.

On one of these weekends, the girls ate their spaghetti at the glass-topped table with straight backs and careful hands.

"Why are you so quiet?" My voice held the tease of the playing and running and laughing we'd been doing all afternoon.

"Mom told us to make sure we were good," they said. "Especially to make sure we don't spill on your white carpet."

It surprised me that my sister saw me this way, or saw my house as one that required special behavior. Was this a story about a childless woman?

I wouldn't have cared. I might have had precious things, but I would have spilled sauce on top of whatever they spilled, to show them I didn't care. Rubbed it in, danced on it, made a game of it.

I thought I'd be a good mother. Kind and fun, loving and patient.

But still. No mother could always be this.

Even though these weekends were full of fun and excitement, there were times when I felt the every-watchful-moment exhaustion. The need to keep them safe and contented, entertained and fed, hair-brushed and tooth-brushed and hydrated. Sometimes I felt tired of these needing children. How did other women do this with no end? How had Mom done it with five kids?

When I was a girl, the chaos filled our big house: TV up loud, toys and papers and dust, Cris crying, us kids whining that we were bored or bickering over a card game or space on the sofa or for no reason at all.

Sometimes Mom yelled at us to *stop, stop, stop. Be quiet.* She said it again and again, and we kept going. Poking and giggling, picking and pushing, screaming and crying. And Mom grew fierce. She screamed. She beat the counter with the rubber spatula, reminding us of its sting on our bare butts. We scattered like quail caught out on the road.

At other times, in the middle of our mess and demand and childish meanness, she went silent. She walked to the living room window like we weren't even there, put her folded arms on the windowpane and rested her head on the angle of her forearms, and looked off toward town or the sky, or somewhere beyond us. It was like she was looking toward another possible life, a life she missed, dreams that didn't include us.

Now, with these needy child-guests in my house, my temporary family, I questioned my own capacity. Maybe I was where I wanted to be: a woman with other people's children. Maybe I was living the kind of life Mom sometimes imagined in her silent moments at that window.

At the end of those weekends, I brought the children back safe. Their arms and legs, their fine skin, bright hearts. I gave them back to their mother, put their bags back in her car, gave hugs goodbye, and got in my own car.

I felt a mixture of sadness and relief. I had to let them go and I would miss them. But I was on my own again. I breathed a breath of relief as I shut my door and pulled out of the parking lot. I rolled down my window and waved at them, waved until they were out of sight. Then I drove home with the wind coming in, the stereo on loud.

39. CRAZY MAZES

CHECK MARKS UNDER TWO columns of a mind's-eye list of why I should push Bill and why I shouldn't:

He would be a wonderful father.

He would be a terrible father.

ON A WEEKEND WHEN Annilee and Shannon visited, Bill played full-force through the first afternoon, the first evening, the next morning. He pretend-juggled boiled eggs that dropped and cracked on the floor, cooked his special spaghetti at night, special pancakes in the morning. Annilee curled up next to him on the sofa when we watched movies. Her love settled on him. He stayed completely still so he didn't disturb her sleepy eyes, her arm resting on his leg.

Wonderful. Check mark.

It all went well until late the next morning, when he got tired and we wanted to keep playing. Until he had a headache. His body was ten years older than mine. In his mid-forties, his health was not always good. Even without children, there were times he needed to have a rest, when his stomach was upset, when his back hurt.

The girls and I played cards quiet while we waited for him. Him stretched out on the sofa, arm over eyes. Whisper cards.

Go Fish, Old Maid. "When will Uncle Bill be ready to play again?" the girls asked.

"Pretty soon." I felt as disappointed as they were. How could he go from such big fun to such big tired?

Terrible. Check mark.

After his rest we all went fun again until six holes into a game of putt-putt golf. Small dimpled balls through crazy mazes. Until Annilee missed three times in a row and Bill said in a hard voice, "Pay attention, you aren't trying hard enough." Her chin trembled, and her trusting heart went to a lower flame.

I didn't put myself between them. I was perky and extra careful with Annilee. Said, "It's okay. You're doing great. This is just for fun." Maybe later he even apologized to her. Maybe she even hit the ball, hole-in-one. I don't remember.

Was this how it would feel to share a child of our own? Would he be hard discipline coach and I be comfort? Would that be the awful tension between us? Me too easy. Him too hard. The child in the middle.

AT NIGHT, AFTER I tucked the girls into the bed in the guest room and crawled into bed with Bill, he wrapped his arms around me. "I love watching you," he said. "You have so much fun with them."

I wished his next words would be: *I love it so much that I want to have our own.* But there were no next words.

Terrible.

I felt a relief in the absence of these wished words. That he was taking the burden of the choice from me, because I had my doubts.

Wonderful.

40. I WAS ALMOST SURE

DAD'S FACE WAS SLACK with his second gin and tonic in the low lights of the Elks Lodge. "Don't you want something to drink, babe?" he said.

It was 1982, and Sam and I were in Condon for the weekend. We'd come out to the Elks for dinner and drinks with Mom and Dad, Leanne and her husband, and Brad. All of us, like grown-ups.

"I'll have another water," I said. All the week before, back in Eugene, I'd walked gently, held the kindest thoughts. I might be pregnant. Now, here with my family, I felt like I had a special secret.

Leanne looked at me and tipped her head to the side, like a question. Me not having a beer. She was out for the first time since her second daughter, Shannon, had been born. "It's hard," she'd told me earlier. "Leaving her for the first time." Part of her always turned in the direction of her girls.

I leaned in toward her, close enough to whisper. "We've been trying."

My period was a few days late. The timing was right, I was almost sure. But since stopping the pill, my cycle hadn't followed an exact schedule, and my old sense of knowing when I was ovulating had faded.

I didn't tell Leanne my worries about how Sam and I would afford a baby. Didn't speak of my secret standoff about who would stay home.

THE BLOOD CAME A few days after that visit to Condon. At first, the disappointment took over. So different from the relief I'd felt when I was a girl and waited to bleed. So different from the relief when I thought I might be pregnant with the cowboy. Maybe getting pregnant wouldn't be as easy for me as it had been for Leanne.

As the days went by, the disappointment flowed away with the blood. Questions stepped into the empty space. Why did I think we could have a child when we could barely afford to pay our bills? What had happened to the girl who wanted a career? How could I justify all that college, the loans I still paid for each month, the hard work I'd put in at the job I loved if all I wanted was to stay at home with a baby? Did I want a baby if I couldn't stay home with it like Leanne, if I couldn't have everything be picture perfect?

III.
A KIND OF
TRANSFORMATION

41. WHAT WE KNEW BY NOW

BILL AND I HAD been married five years, six, seven, and if people wondered whether we would have children, they didn't ask. As time went on, it was clear we were a couple who traveled. In the space where they might have asked about our kids, now they asked about our travels.

In the stress and joy of traveling, Bill and I became a team. We had our routines. Bill saying, "How would you like to go to (Glacier, Banff, Yellowstone, the Desert Southwest, Mexico, the Olympics, Egypt, Greece, Switzerland)?" Me saying, "Yes."

He did the planning (reading books and making notes and buying tickets, mapping routes and best tours, hikes, campgrounds, hotels, restaurants). I did the packing (imagining being there with sun, snow, rain, hike, picnic lunch, busy market, bug, snake, burn, pickpocket), and thinking of every little thing either of us would need so if Bill asked, "Where is the (battery, tweezers, aspirin, ointment, notebook, peanut butter, Pepto Bismol)?" I'd be able to say, "It's right here."

We had an airplane routine (book, pencil, crossword, water, tickets in this bag, check that bag), and a car routine (you drive three hours, I drive three hours, map in the place next to the passenger, save your nap for driving through southern Idaho), a camping routine in our little pop-up tent-trailer (I take out the poles, he unhitches from the car, he does the campfire food, I do the cooktop food), and a hiking routine (start early, have lunch, one PB&J, one cheddar cheese warmed from the sun, come back to camp, shower, make love, nap).

Bill knew by now that I would try anything (on a hike up Angel's Landing in Zion National Park, the last half mile along the narrow rock fin, chains to hold on the side of the sheer 1500-foot drop, and I was scared and I wouldn't stop, because giving up would be worse than going on). I knew he would come for me when I was scared and hadn't told him that I didn't know how to do a thing (me thinking, *what could be hard about snorkeling in the ocean in Mexico?* Him giving me mask and fins and taking off ahead of me. The current pulled me in another direction, toward the rocks, and I didn't know how to breathe with this thing in my mouth and this mask not sealed on my face and I choked and panicked and he turned back for me, held me in the water, took me to shore, whispered, "It's okay, it's okay, it's okay").

When we became separated (in the flower market, spice market, supermercado, church, museum, airport, busy street, hiking trail), I looked for Bill's curly head, tall over people and trees and sandstone rocks. Curly pepper with salt and, as time went by, curly salt with pepper. The steady level way he held his head.

We knew there would be a fight (I am too hungry, he is too tired, I think it's the road-trail-street to the right, he thinks it's the road-trail-street to the left). And we trusted we would find our way through it. We would speak with hurt and then not speak for some hours, and then reach out (my hand or his) and reach back (his hand or mine), and we would talk and learn something new that changed how we entered the fight and how we found our way out.

Every trip was a trial and test and love, and we were at our best the more hours we had together. Every trip Bill planned was a gift held out to me, the adventure he could give me. Every trip I said yes to was my gift held out to him (I will go with you to places that scare me and amaze me and teach me and draw me even closer to you). We knew we would do this for the rest of our lives.

When we went to Bill's mother's house after a trip, to give her a necklace or charm we had found for her, she would come running out the door, arms wide, calling out, "My Billie's home, my Billie's home," and wrap those arms around him and then around me. And in this moment, I would see his happiness with her, and how his love for her had shaped his capacity to love me.

We saved the addresses of the people we'd met on our travels. A family from Switzerland had two children who wanted to learn to speak English so we could all talk together.

In Greece, we met a couple from England who were there to get married. They asked us to stand in as witnesses because they hadn't come with anyone from home and we seemed like the kind of people who would remember their day. In the southwest desert, we met a couple from Georgia who traveled to the desert every year because they loved it as much as we did. We stayed in contact with these people from other places, and the tendrils of friendship and love spanned thousands of miles.

On visits to Condon after our travels, we came with pictures and stories, a new shirt for Dad, a necklace for Mom, and gifts for the kids until there were so many kids we would need a whole other suitcase, and so we stopped. When we ran into the people of Condon, they asked where we'd traveled to last, where we planned to go next.

42. THE THINGS PEOPLE THINK

BILL SAT NEXT TO me at a dinner party, talking to the man on his other side, not hearing the question that the woman across from me asked.

Do you have kids?

How many times had I been asked this in the seven years since Bill and I married? Ten? Thirty? Sixty? Asked by the man next to me on a plane, the new co-worker, the dental hygienist at the dentist office right before I opened wide. Asked in the same way people who don't know you might ask, "What do you do? Where are you from?" An icebreaker, a get-to-know-you, let's-find-something-in-common question.

This woman asked it in the same way as all the others, her eyes on me, sure I would say, *yes I do*, that I would tell how many, their names, show pictures. The ice would be broken.

"No," I said. I took a quick breath, rushing to get the rest of my story in before she could think what she might think of a woman with no children.

"No, we don't have kids. We love them. But." I smiled. I touched Bill's hand even though he wasn't listening, so she would know: I have love, I am happy. "We decided not to have them. Bill didn't want to be an older father. We met a little too late. We spend lots of time with our nieces and nephews. Spoil them. Get them all wound up and send them home. We get all the good parts."

I filled the space between us with words before different words came to her mind: Selfish. Self-centered. Odd. Barren. Lonely. Bitter.

"How about you?" I asked.

I knew how to talk to people about their kids. And they almost always had kids or planned to, or were trying, or their children were having children. I could speak of pregnancy and feeding, rolling over and solid foods and nap times. And, as the kids in my life got older, I could speak of T-ball and learning styles, and crafts for six-year-olds, how to help an eight-year-old with her fears, a ten-year-old with a science project.

I knew these things. I had done these things.

But this woman next to me at the dinner party said, "No." She almost winked, as if we were part of a secret club. "I've never wanted children."

Sometimes a question is only a question.

43. THE SYMBOLS OF MY NAME

WHEN BILL AND I traveled, I calculated time zones to leave no chance of an egg being released. At the right time each day, sometimes morning, sometimes night, I took out the round packet and pressed a tiny yellow pill through thin tinfoil. I placed the pill on my tongue, drank water, swallowed it down. Then Bill and I went out to see the world or slipped into bed and made love in a new place.

Mom had once told me she knew when she conceived each of us kids. How could this be? Were these the moments when she decided to not use the usual protections? Were the moments of sexual intimacy between her and Dad so rare that she remembered each? Did she know her body so well, like I once thought I knew mine?

In Luxor, Egypt, Bill and I walked through the columns at Karnak Temple. The tour guide showed us a statue of a giant scarab beetle. He told us the scarab was an ancient sacred symbol of fertility. He told us it would bring a baby if we walked around it counter-clockwise seven times.

Maybe this man told other people it would bring health or

prosperity or luck, but he told us it would bring a child. We looked like a couple in love, and a couple in love must want a child.

I laughed and stepped away. I felt the usual spotlight embarrassment that came with the expectations of others as they pointed at the prescribed path that led to children.

But, on this day, in this place, I was where I wanted to be. If, after learning of Mom's disappointment, I had said we must have a child or else, I would not have been here now, on this adventure.

I did not walk around the scarab counter-clockwise seven times.

In Cairo, a driver drove Bill and me through the center of the city, tall stone buildings, laundry drying from windows. Cars honked and traffic went this way, that way. In the middle of an eight-lane road, a group of men dressed in white carried a small coffin, also white, through traffic. They carried the coffin on their shoulders. The traffic moved around them. A child had died. I thought of the mothers. The grandmothers, the aunts. They were somewhere else, holding their burden in a private place.

Back home I gave silver cartouche pendants to our nieces, each with her name spelled out in hieroglyph enclosed in a long oval. I kept one for myself, with the symbols of my name in gold: a cobra, an eagle, a basket, and double slashes. At the bottom was another symbol, a scarab.

Back home I looked up the story of the scarab. For some, the celebration of the scarab is the glorification of birth. For others, the scarab is seen as having the power to emerge after a period of hiding.

The sacred scarab is a dung beetle. The beetle rolls dung into balls and buries these balls in the earth. The dung is used by the beetles for food and to nourish the eggs they lay in it. When the young scarabs hatch, they come up from the earth. They look like small dark suns rising in the same way the sun appears to come from the earth on the eastern horizon. A transformation that is not what it seems.

44. THIS WAS NEW. THIS WAS SCARY. I WANTED MORE.

EVEN AFTER THE BLOOD came, and even though I still worried what would happen if I got pregnant, Sam and I were still trying early in 1983 when a woman at work told me about a class she'd taken.

"I think you'd like it," she said. "It's a way of really getting honest with yourself."

I looked at her.

"Personal growth," she said. "They help you look at your life, make sure you're living it to your fullest, that you're not going through it half asleep."

I didn't know what she meant, but she had a new brightness in her eyes, a confidence in her voice.

"I can't really explain it," she said. "All I can tell you is it will change your life."

I told Sam about the classes, five days of long hours. I wanted to go. He said, sure, go. No, he didn't want to join me.

I signed up.

THE LEADERS, TWO MEN in their early thirties, slim with styled hair and expensive dark suits, sat on tall chairs at the front of the room. They spoke into handheld microphones. There were a hundred of us, the participants. We sat on metal folding chairs arranged in precise rows. I was in an aisle seat. The chairs were close together; my shoulder touched the woman next to me. I moved my chair a few inches away from her.

One leader said, "We want you to pay attention to what you agree to and the strength of your intention to keep that agreement. Think about this, especially in terms of the agreements you make to yourself."

The other leader asked everyone to stand. He said, "Here are the agreements you must make to participate in this class."

With each agreement we were to sit if we agreed, keep standing if we didn't.

"Be on time. You will not be let in if you are late. If you miss a session, you will be dropped from the program."

I sat. This would not be a problem. I was always early. A man and a woman stayed standing.

A discussion followed. The man sat, the woman sat. We all stood again.

"Do not leave the room until we give you a break. Even to use the bathroom."

I sat. I would drink less water. Three women stayed standing.

A discussion followed. The women sat.

"No food or drinks or gum in the room."

I sat.

"Don't move your chair from the position it is in when you arrive. Unless we ask you to move it for an exercise."

I stayed standing.

People turned in their chairs, looked at me the same way I'd looked at the three woman who didn't want to wait for breaks to use the bathroom. "I have a small bladder," one woman had said. They looked at me the same way I'd looked at the man who'd said he might have to be late because of work. The way I'd looked at the woman who'd asked, "What if my car breaks down? I can't help that."

A woman with a flowy skirt moved down the aisle toward me, microphone in her hand. She handed me the microphone.

The leader asked me, "Why don't you agree to keep your chair where we've placed it?"

The microphone was heavy. I spoke into it. "I don't like to sit close to people." My voice everywhere in the room. My chair at a slant behind me.

"Why?" the leader asked.

Mom used to joke about my great aunts who always wanted a hug and a kiss. One night when I was six or seven or eight she said I was old enough to not kiss her good night anymore. That was the last time I'd kissed her or hugged her. Now being hugged made me uncomfortable. Since the rape, even more so.

I spoke into the microphone. "I don't think you should be able to tell me how close I have to sit to someone." An edge to my voice. "I don't see the big deal about moving my chair a little."

"This is about challenging your self-limiting beliefs," the leaders had said to a woman who didn't want to wait to pee.

"This is about keeping your agreements," they'd said to the man who might be late. "You signed up for this class knowing the hours. You made a commitment to yourself. How often do you say you will do something knowing you might not?"

"This is about being accountable," they'd said to the woman whose car might break down. "It's time to decide what you want in your life and stop blaming others for not having it."

"This is about your getting out of your comfort zone," one leader said to me. "And your comfort zone may not be as comfortable as you think," the other leader said to me. "This is about challenging the stories you have about yourself. We act on our stories without ever questioning whether they are still true."

A rush, a flush on my face. Like they knew me, cared about me, cared what kind of life I had.

This was new. This was scary. I wanted more.

"Are you willing to be challenged?" they asked me.

"Yes." I moved my chair back to its place. I sat. I folded my arms, tucked my shoulders in so I wouldn't brush against the woman next to me.

AROUND ME, MEN, WOMEN, young and old sat in chairs, facing each other. Knees close, hands in laps. My partner for this exercise, a woman a few years older, sat across from me. "Look at each other," the leaders had said. "Don't speak." I looked at her face. Her nose was uneven. Her eyes were blue. Her eyes. On mine. I breathed. I worried what she would see, my big pores, stray hair on my eyebrows, acne scars on my cheeks. "Stay with it," the leaders said. "Let your partner see you. See them."

The flight in my stomach, my chest.

Her eyes. Something there. She wasn't her face. I wasn't mine. I was more. She was more.

"Now one of you begin speaking. But say something new. Something you've never told anyone before."

"This is hard for me," I said. "To just sit. To not talk. To look at you and have you look at me."

"I know," she said. "But when I look at you, I see beauty. I see hurt. I see strength."

This was new. This was scary. I wanted more.

I didn't think I could dance. They put on music, the Pointer Sisters singing "Jump," and they said, "Dance like your life depends on it." I danced. It didn't matter if I was good.

It was as though I'd been stirred from a long sleep where I'd been dreaming a dream of someone else's life. I woke from that other person's dream knowing I wanted something different.

They made a line of people, and I could decide who came close, and who didn't, choose which person I hugged and which I didn't. I wrapped my arms around almost all.

Like soil long-parched by sun, each new thing was fresh rain, sinking into cracks and crevices.

Live as if death is on your left shoulder, they said.

This sat me up, and I moved toward these words.

This isn't a dress rehearsal, they said.

Like from water and sun, that seed of knowing, planted and buried four years earlier in the dangerous morning hours with a stranger, grew to life. How easy it is to die. The urgency to be present, take in each moment. Be alive.

All the possibilities for me to choose were open. I wanted more. I wanted different from what I had.

But how would I know I was choosing right?

SAM STAYED AT HOME, writing or reading with a glass of bourbon or a cup of coffee. I came from a session or from getting together with my new friends, carrying all the excitement on me. I'd signed up for the next class. The second level. "Come with me," I said to him. "You can do the first one and catch up."

He didn't want to go. He didn't like the change in me. Maybe I was being brainwashed.

I went to the second level. Sam stayed home. I was gone all day, much of the night, only home for sleep, to change clothes. The lights of our townhouse seemed dull and flat. I woke in the night to the shifting inside me. Telling him about the possibilities of me that I hadn't known.

He called my parents, told them I was taking these courses. He told them they were filling my head with things. I might be involved with a cult. They must have been scared. Not far from Condon, Rajneeshpuram had sprung up near the town of Antelope. People wearing red clothes, dancing naked. Hugging at random. *Cult,* everyone said.

I called my parents and told them not to worry. Everything was okay.

I told Sam that they were filling my head with good things. "I wasn't happy. I didn't know it, but I wasn't. But I am now." I told him I hadn't liked myself much, and I did now.

He had thought I was happy before. I had thought so too.

"Come with me," I asked him again.

He was glad I was happy. He didn't feel the need to change himself.

THE NEXT TIME I called Mom, I said, "I love you." Years, maybe, since I had said that. Had I ever said it?

A pause. "I love you too," she said. Natural, like she'd been waiting for me.

The next time I saw Dad, I hugged him hello and, the next time after that, he put his arms around me, and I leaned into him. He hadn't held me since I was a girl of seventeen and had sat on his lap that early morning after the prom.

He'd stopped drinking earlier in the year, after his doctor told him it would be a good idea. Though it may have been hard for him privately, from the outside, it seemed like an easy change. He made the decision and he quit.

Now the time and attention he'd put to drinking was given to his grandkids. He related to them with a quiet presence I remembered from when I was a little girl and had walked with him in the cold winter nights to feed the bummer lambs.

THE LEADERS HAD US stand. They said, "Find the person in the room that you have the most resistance to." I looked at a tall, thin woman with curly hair, pale skin, and glasses. Earlier I'd heard her say, "I don't have children and I don't want to have children." She'd said it with her chin up, straight out, no apology. I couldn't imagine. Why wouldn't a woman want children?

"Go to that person and tell them what it is you resist in them."

People moved around the room, finding the person. I went straight to her.

We stood facing each other. I said, "I feel uncomfortable around you. I think you are selfish not wanting children."

She said, "Okay." She smiled an open smile, even against my harsh words. She said. "Are you curious about why I don't want children?"

The lights in the room were low. All around us, pairs of people stood saying why they were not drawn to each other.

"Okay. Why?" I said. Ready to shoot down every reason she had. Because a woman should want to have children.

She said, "A lot of women have children because they think it will make them happy. I don't want to have a child to make me happy. I'm happy as I am. There are enough children. I don't need one of my own." She looked at me. Sam and I hadn't stopped trying to have a child. "Let me ask you. Why do you want to have a child?"

I wanted a child because having children was what women did. And even though it's what they all did, it made them special. I wanted the attention. The baby shower, the baby clothes, the story of the birth. The child to hold and love. I would be a good mom. A child would make me happy. I wanted a child because I'd never considered not having one.

None of those reasons seemed good enough now.

45. AN UGLY, MESSY, HURTFUL THING

Maybe if I hadn't taken those classes. Or if I'd gotten pregnant and couldn't go to the classes. Maybe if I hadn't met a new man in those classes. If I'd paid attention to what they taught about keeping agreements. Maybe I would have stayed with Sam longer. Maybe I would have stayed forever.

The classes opened me to a new way of seeing the world. Opened me to a new way of being in the world. The classes weren't set up to protect the world I already lived in. I wanted a different kind of life than the one I'd set in place before I even considered all the possible ways of living.

Sam couldn't understand. Why couldn't we go back to the way we had been?

I was still in love with falling in love. Old habits are hard to break, especially when you can't recognize them as habit. The new man, Stephen, was unlike anyone I'd ever let myself want. And I wanted him. I couldn't see that he was another on my well-worn path of falling in love and falling out of love. A distraction from myself and my insecurities and needs.

It took months for me to leave Sam. My leaving was ugly, messy, hurtful. Knowing I wanted to go but not being able to put into words why. No answer would have satisfied Sam. No answer would have made my leaving easier for him.

I tried all the things I'd learned in those classes.

Honesty. "There's a man I'm attracted to." Stephen was one of the assistants in the classes. Tall and handsome, and he looked at me like I was someone new.

Integrity. "We haven't done anything. I just wanted to tell you how I feel." We hadn't done anything, that man and I. Not yet. But we talked about it. We met in private. The wanting made it almost as good as the having.

Accountability. "Okay. I won't leave." I'd made an agreement to be Sam's wife, before I knew what an agreement was. I would stay and try to find my love for Sam. But I stopped trying to have a baby and started taking the birth control pills again.

Manipulation. Something they hadn't taught me in those classes, but I knew anyway. "I'm telling you the truth; I'm just being honest. I'm attracted to someone else, but that's not the reason I want to leave." The truth as I saw it then.

Silence. Let the marriage go flat and dry.

Presence. "Live your life as if death is at your left shoulder." That seed of knowledge germinating. Life can end in a moment. Yes, there was another man. That is not why I needed to leave.

Six months went by.

"It's over," I told Sam. Not even four years married.

I WENT HOME TO tell my parents. Harvest was underway, with Brad operating the combine and Dad running the trucks. I rode with Dad one afternoon, and in between loads, we sat in the shade of the truck while we waited for the combine to come around.

Dad rested his back against the tire. Stretched his legs out on the powder dust left from the tire tracks of combine and truck. "Did he hit you?" he asked. "Was he having an affair?" Trying to make sense of my leaving Sam. "Is there another man?"

"No," I said. "It's hard to explain. I don't want to be with him anymore."

"We don't get divorces in this family." Dad was stunned the way Sam had been stunned. I had stunned myself with my sudden turn from wife to not wife.

A burlap bag hung from the bed of the truck. The bag, damp and cool, held water for the driver. As a girl, when I rode with Dad, I drank the cool water from that bag, let it clear the dry dust of my mouth.

Now, even though it was hot and my mouth was dry, I didn't take a drink. A small withholding for the pain I'd caused Sam, the worry I had once again become to my parents.

46. CONDITIONAL SURRENDER

"Let's freeze some of your sperm," I joked with Bill. "If you die first and I'm young enough, I could have your child, but you wouldn't have to raise it. It would be like having a part of you still here. A little Billie."

Or, after him, there might be another man. Not as good in a thousand ways except for this: he would want a child.

I didn't want another man. I wanted Bill.

He touched my face and kissed me. He didn't think I was serious. I didn't know if I was serious.

That little boy, with his dark eyes and black curls, would hold my hand as we walked, he would look up at me and ask about his dad. *He would have loved you,* I'd say.

I was thirty-four, thirty-five, thirty-seven. My periods trickled off from five days to three, three to one. The pills stopping what a woman's body can do. And then only for a day, that fourth Tuesday. A mention, a spot of blood, a small monthly reminder that there might still be a chance.

Sometimes I looked at my tidy end-of-workday desk, projects complete, files filed, and the missing pressed in. An uncried cry in my throat, chest, gut. *Why am I here? If not for a child then what will I be for?*

Bill didn't take a last step. Vasectomy. I didn't want him to. And for me there would be no tubal ligation like my friend Bonnie, who had told me over lunch those years ago that this was her plan, and then she did it. Other women might be sure enough for this final cutting of possibility. I was not.

Bill could change his mind. Wake one morning from a dream of fatherhood and say, "We must. Now, before it's too late."

But he wasn't that man. He wouldn't change his mind without me changing it.

Once, I did.

I asked, "Don't you want a baby with me?" For the twentieth or thirty-seventh or ninety-first time. My voice was innocent, forced-perky. Pleading thinly veiled.

Bill said, in a giving up voice, "Okay, Jackie."

My breath held. I didn't know if he meant it. He must have been worn down, exhausted by my ambush questions.

"I'm tired of this," he said. "And I don't want you to blame me for saying no. If you really want a child, then okay."

The strings were attached in the short pause between what he said first and what he said next.

"But I'm going to retire in a few years." His steady career and the early retirement he could take for the toll of being a firefighter. "If we have a child, you'll have to work longer than you planned." His voice was calm, but I could hear the frayed edges of having to repeat this plan to me, the fear that I might push so hard he had to give it up. He said, "I want to travel. It'll be harder for you to go. You'd have to be okay with me going without you."

His conditional surrender trapped me in a box canyon. Surrounded by my wants, his limits.

To have a child with this man who felt the burden of it before it even arrived meant passing on the unfinished legacy of Bill's father. From father to Bill, from Bill to child.

And anyway, he didn't mean okay, I was sure.

But what if?

My romance of a perfect stay-at-home motherhood was rigid. His conditions revealed my own. I wanted him to share the joy of trying, the expectancy, the naming and welcoming, the parenting. I wanted him with me on all of it, one hundred percent. I wanted to be a mother under the easiest of circumstances, or no motherhood at all.

The limits to my own wanting embarrassed me. The only way out was to go back the way I'd come. My surrender.

I stopped asking Bill why he didn't want children and followed the trail of my own motivations, the yearning for what I didn't have. Yes, I loved children. I believed what women said about the powerful love and sacrifice you only know when you have a child of your own. Yes, at times, my body called out to be filled with child, to know what birth was like.

But my body also called out for other possibilities that I didn't pursue: to run a marathon, to climb the face of a cliff, to go beyond my limits. My longings always called out for more, more, more than what I had.

And I kept opening the same wound over and over, thinking a child would be the salve. I wanted Mom's approval. I wanted the approval of the women in the mothering club. I didn't like to be left out. I didn't want to be pitied. Or judged.

Maybe this thing I called wanting a child was a distraction from a bigger need: to understand why I was here, why I was alive. My need to justify myself.

Would a child justify me?

Would it make me happy?

Wasn't I already happy?

I had the life I had because of the absence of a child. Bill and I were free to explore each other and ourselves in uninterrupted time.

In wanting this one thing that I didn't have, I was squandering what I did have. Here was the rising of that seed of knowledge I had taken in all those years ago when I was raped. *Death can come at any moment. Be present, or you will miss your life.*

47. THE PLACE WHERE UNGIVEN LOVE IS HELD

LIFE MADE A PATH around the wanting.

I was the birthday rememberer, the gift giver, the card sender, the one who knows every gesture to the "Little Bunny Foo Foo" song. I was the weekend entertainer: *Movies! Arcades! Putt-putt golf! Bubbles!* I was the one cheering on the sidelines. The one to dance, to giggle, to put on her bathing suit and slip and slide on the banana slide, try the roller blades, the skateboard, be silly in a way a mother can't always be.

I was the listener for mothers who worried. The listener to their children too.

Annilee, at eight on an overnight at our house, tells me her struggles with making mistakes in her schoolwork and getting mad. I say, "It's okay to get mad." And I say more about perfection and that anger is normal, but it's what we do with it that's important. She says, "Oh," and then she tells me the whole plot of a movie she loved. Later, Leanne says, "Thank you. She told me you said it was okay. Even though I told her that too. It meant something coming from you."

Raphael, the fifteen-year-old son of our Swiss friends, shares his first broken heart while we hike in the Alps. I tell him about the care we must take with broken hearts, and later his mother says she's relieved he talked to me because he's been so quiet. Many years later he will invite us to his wedding and seat Bill and me at the head table and call us his American parents.

His sister Jessica, at five, stares up at my long dark hair and said, *"Elle est belle,"* and I feel beautiful. At sixteen she asks to live with us for a summer so she can practice her English and begins to speak with me of more than the simple things.

Our niece Christy is sixteen when her mom calls and says, "Please come and talk to her. Something has happened and she won't tell me." I go to her house and her mother lets me in. I knock on her bedroom door, and Christy lets me in. We sit on the edge of her bed. She tells me about what has happened, what has hurt her, and then we go to her mother.

Our nephew Jared is eight when asked to rate his day on a scale of one to ten, and he says, "You mean I get to pick?" I nod, as surprised by this idea as he is. I say, "Yes, of course, you decide." He says, "It's a ten. Why wouldn't every day be a ten?"

Why wouldn't it? I get to pick.

"I WANT A NEW job," I said.

"Yes," Bill said. "Do it."

"I want to cut back on work and go to school for a master's degree."

"Yes! Go for it."

"Let's take that class together."

"Let's teach this class together."

"Let's build a house."

"Yes! Let's do it."

When I was absolutely sure about what I wanted, Bill was all in too. He met my enthusiasm, celebrated my clarity.

IN 1995, WE MOVED into the house of my design with two bedrooms, and a great room with windows that took full advantage of the view to the old cedars out back.

Two of Bill's aunts whispered and nodded when they saw

the small alcove off the master bedroom. "This would be a good room for a baby." We had already filled that room: treadmill, stationary bike, free weights.

I picked a cupboard in the great room for toys and books and crayons and paper, stickers and glitter and glue. *This is where the fun starts!* The front of our refrigerator filled with drawings and school pictures until the magnets could not hold.

Now it was Cris's girls, Alyson and Devin, who came from Condon for weekend visits. The sound of these two laughing together filled the rooms of our new home.

We'd designed the house with a private space for guests. Over the years, nieces and nephews grew to young adulthood and would need a place to stay while they worked a city summer job before college, or saved for their own place. They would use this space for temporary living, and we would become a temporary family.

AT NIGHT WE STOOD in the bathroom before the big mirror. Me at my sink, Bill at his. We brushed our teeth. I ran water on my face, took a towel to pat it dry. Looked at us in the mirror. His hair grayer. Small lines around my eyes.

"It's probably good we didn't have kids," I said. "That poor baby's nose."

He stopped brushing, "What?" He looked worried. This again.

I was showing him, *it's okay.* "Each of us on our own, our noses are just prominent." *You see, I can even joke about it now.* "But if you put us together, that kid could have had a honker."

THE DESIRE AGED AND shifted in me. I was thirty-nine, forty, forty-one. My arms had once wanted an infant to hold; now my legs wanted a toddler to chase; then it was a longing for a five-year-old learning to make jokes, a ten-year-old speaking logic, a twelve-year-old awkward and still wanting to play. Each age became the age I loved best.

The child I didn't have grew in this place of possibility, the place where ungiven love is held. Here also, I kept a part of myself back from Bill, the part that could have witnessed him as a father, been witnessed as a mother. My ungiven love wrapped tightly around a stone of resentment that rested on one side of a scale, hidden even from myself: a scale that measured who had done more, who had given up more for the other.

48. THE HEART OF A WITNESS

Announcements came in the mail with pictures of nearly grown kids leaning against tree trunks or hay bales or standing in parks with ponds in the background. Invitations in swirly lettering asked us to witness the graduation march of our nieces and nephews.

Yes, Bill and I said, of course. We would love to.

Through the mid-nineties and for years beyond, we sat with family on bleachers in shiny-floored gymnasiums or football fields while Tawna, JD, Carrie Sue, David, Eric, Annilee, Shannon, Amber, Jared, Alyson, Joely, and the others that came after, took their diplomas, shook hands with principals, wore gowns and tassels, and gave smiles and hugs for pictures.

"It's hard," one mother said after the ceremony. "My kids have been the focus of everything I do." She looked around to her right, to her left, like she was looking for the toddlers her children used to be.

I felt compassion for her. The struggle she faced was akin to what I'd been exploring for years: *Who will I be without children?* I felt smug with the idea that I'd trekked further along in the search. The years she'd been distracted with kids, I'd had to meet myself without.

•

WHILE I HAD A taste, by proximity, of what it is like to shepherd children to the moments of letting go, one thing I could not know was the experience of giving birth. The mystery of it still compelled me, drew my eyes to each pregnant woman, kept me listening to stories of birth.

I'd known our niece Christy, Bill's brother's daughter, since she was ten. Now she was twenty and pregnant. This baby would make me a great-aunt for the first time.

Like my great aunt Lena.

I was thirty-eight years old. I wasn't lonely. I wasn't bitter.

Christy needed all the help she could get. Though she and the father of the baby were on good terms, they were no longer a couple.

I hosted a baby shower for her. Invitations and balloons and a decorated cake with pink rattles, paper plates and napkins with tiny baby carriages.

Women gathered on sofas and chairs in my living room. Christy opened gifts that we passed around the room. Cousins and aunts held up tiny onesies and stuffed toys and said, "Isn't that the cutest?" to each thing.

"I can't wait to hold her," Christy said when she announced the baby would be a girl. "I love babies. I've always loved babies."

So have I, I thought. But her strong desire to have a child overpowered any worries that might stop her. Worries about not being with the father, or what she would need to care for a baby, or how she could afford it. This stunned me. How different we were. I'd always had reasons and worries to balance my wanting.

At the end of the afternoon, we put the baby gifts back in bags and boxes and carried them to the car. Christy said, "I want to ask you something."

I put an armful in the back seat and said, "Uh-huh." Not expecting anything more than maybe she wanted the recipe for the punch, or a ride to the doctor.

"And you can say no if you don't want to."

Now she had my attention.

"Will you be there when the baby comes?"

"Yes," I said. "We both will." In the waiting room. With whoever else would be in the waiting room waiting to hear the baby was born.

"No," Christy said. "Mom can't be there." Her mother lived a few states away. She wouldn't be able to get there in time. "I mean will you be in the room with me?"

The one thing I couldn't know any other way. This was as close as I would get.

Yes. Of course. I'd love to.

EVEN THOUGH I'D SAID yes, I wasn't sure. Maybe it would be too hard. Maybe this would be the time when it hurt, completely hurt. The time when I would know bitterness and regret.

I reminded myself that this was for Christy, not for me. I would be there to help, to support her through the pain and power of bringing life.

A few weeks later she told me her boyfriend would be there too, to coach her. Not the father of the baby but her new boyfriend. I didn't know if she'd known this all along or if this was something new. I asked, did she still want me there?

Yes, she said. I do.

Maybe she'd asked me to be there for me, not for her. Maybe she knew more about me than I thought I'd shown. The missing in me. Was this love and generosity? Was it pity?

It didn't matter. I wanted to see this baby be born.

In the weeks before the birth, I waited for the call. I made myself ready. I packed my heart, as if in a small suitcase of tissue and silk, ready any time to go to the hospital. The heart of a witness.

AT FIRST, IN THE birthing room, time moved slowly. The nurses checked monitors and medication. I watched and asked the nurses questions about monitors and medication. The boyfriend was there. Christy's dad, Clint, and Bill came in for a while. The room was more festive than the usual hospital visit. We were all waiting for the next thing.

When the next thing started, more frequent contractions, the nurse adjusting dials, checking dilation, I didn't know what to do or how to help.

The boyfriend was by Christy's side, holding her hand and cheering her on through each contraction. He would be there for her all the way through; maybe she didn't need me. But she'd asked me to be here. To witness her child coming into the world.

And then it didn't matter because things sped up. Contractions came faster and faster. The doctor came in and sat on a black stool with silver wheels. She wheeled forward to the triangle made by Christy's legs. A mirror was set up so we could all see. But I didn't need to help, and I didn't have to use the mirror. I stayed near the doctor, saw what she saw as Christy pushed and pushed.

It was like births I'd seen on TV, or even more detailed in health class birthing videos in college. Like the calves that had come in winter. Birth follows a pattern. Seeing it here, in real life, didn't seem new or shocking.

But I couldn't take my eyes away.

How the body can open. The mess and the capacity. The blood and mucous. The baby's dark hair came from Christy's swollen pink flesh. The head, the shoulders. What Christy had held for so long, she let go with a sudden, final slipping out, and the baby came.

Birth was awful. Birth was beautiful.

I stayed close by while the doctor clamped the cord; the placenta came, more blood and mess, stitches for Christy. The nurse quick-treated the baby with the immediate things, then placed her on Christy's chest. The baby tucked her legs, like still in the womb, her dark hair slick, her small cry.

A new girl had come into the world. I was in her life from the first moment. Maybe a touch closer to what it might have been like to give birth. But this was not knowing. This was witnessing.

THIS GIRL, M'ARI IS her name, will be in my life as the days go by. One day I will watch her cross the stage for a diploma, watch her mother's dismay that the years went so fast.

But before that, I will walk on an Oregon beach with her. She will be six years old. Her little sister Ariana will be on my other side.

The Pacific Ocean will be blue and gray and white and birds and clouds and fine sand. Foam and salt and rot and wind. Water in and water out. There will be driftwood, and boulders that can be reached only when the tide is out.

M'ari will take my hand. "Let's pretend you're our mom," she'll say.

Yes. Of course. I would love to.

49. ALL OUT, ALL IN, ALL OVER

STEPHEN, THE MAN I was sure was the one, could see into me, all that I was and all of my possibility. He worked for the company that put on those classes. He had big plans for a big life. He was healthy, like I'd become (running and lifting weights, no alcohol, no drugs, no smoking, no sugar, no fats, no meat). This man was for me.

I waited the right amount of time, to avoid breaking one of the rules from those classes (don't have an affair). The right amount of time so the new man didn't break the rule of his job (don't sleep with the participants, especially the married ones). I went to the courthouse and got the divorce papers, filled out the forms, paid the fee. I kept moving fast, to not think about the hurt I'd caused Sam.

I moved in with new friends from the classes. Amy and her then-boyfriend Will had a spare bedroom. They made space in their basement for most of the belongings I'd kept from my marriage. My short life as wife, pushed to a corner and covered with a drop cloth.

The papers came in the mail. May 1985. I was divorced.

"It's final," I said to Stephen. "I'm no longer married. The one-year rule is over."

That first time with him I hardly made it over his doorstep before we were out of our clothes and into each other. That first time made all that waiting almost worth it. In those first weeks we fueled ourselves from our stored up wanting. I saw him on weekends, me driving from Eugene to Portland, where he lived, or meeting somewhere.

One afternoon we met at the coast. The sun shone. But it was early spring, and it was the Oregon coast, which meant cold. We sat in the car and watched the sun diamond the waves, watched the waves come and go, come and go.

He said, "I think I'm falling in love with you."

The quickest briefest wash of worry in my chest; so fast I didn't know what it was, except for this: *Too soon*.

It was cold outside and warm inside. I wanted him to love me. "I think I love you too," I said.

Within six months I quit my job, left Eugene where I'd lived for nine years, and moved North to Portland to live with Stephen.

I barely even gave a nod goodbye to the slow city-town of it, the green, the rain, and hibachi smoke, bicycles and beards and runners. All that had happened there: a degree, a career, a crime, a marriage, a divorce, a transformation.

And yet, when it came to men, nothing had changed.

The day I moved, we rented a small truck. Just the two of us loaded it. I couldn't fit all my belongings in, and I left most of Aunt Lena's things behind with my friend Amy, saying I would get them sometime. An oak desk, a mirrored china cabinet, the rocking chair Leanne had wanted. I didn't think to ask her if she wanted it now.

Within a few months Stephen said, "I love you, but you're not the one."

I didn't see it coming.

"Why?" Calm outside, the surprise of it made me still. Pain inside, the heat in my stomach, the stab of his words spreading.

Stephen didn't have an answer. Not the kind that I could

do anything about. "It's a feeling I get," he said. "You're not the one I'm going to spend my life with."

I said, "I love you. You are the one."

I would make him see it.

At first I was reasonable.

AT HOME IN CONDON, I pretended everything was okay. I didn't want to worry my family. I didn't want them to think Stephen was just another man. In my life. Out of my life.

On my visits home, Leanne and her husband came out to the ranch with their girls. Annilee was five, Shannon was three. They thought I was magic. I laughed and ran and danced with them. They liked that I played silly, that I made funny voices and crazy faces. I ran in the sprinklers and brought gifts and let them ride on my back like a horse.

"Do you know what?" I said. "Do you know I can make myself invisible?" They looked at me with hopeful eyes.

"No, you can't," Shannon said. Already her eyes were on my hands, my legs, my face, to see if any part of me had disappeared yet.

"Yes, I can."

"Show us." Annilee clapped her hands.

NOTHING CHANGED STEPHEN'S MIND.

I became unreasonable.

Once a month, once a week, once a day, once an hour. I asked. I asked. I asked. I asked.

"Has it changed?"

"Do you know now I am the one for you?"

"Why aren't I the one?"

"What can I do?"

I read every book he talked about. I bought new clothes, higher heels, stockings and garter belts. I ran more. Lifted weights more. Ate less. He talked about pregnant women being sexy, and he wanted a child someday. Even though I'd let go of the blind need for a child, I could still have one.

His romance ignited mine. I imagined our infant in his arms; downy head resting in his open palm, the length of that baby along his forearm.

In less than a year he moved out.

"I love you," he said. "But I'm not in love with you."

Words spoken a thousand times by a thousand lovers. Words spoken by me to Sam. But never to me. Not until now.

"YOU HAVE TO CLOSE your eyes," I said. "And you have to sit really still."

The girls closed their eyes. Dark long lashes against pale child skin.

"No peeking," I said.

They put their child hands over their eyes.

Mom and Dad were watching.

Leanne smiled.

I went into the kitchen, tiptoe quiet.

Leanne said, "Oh, wow. Aunt Jackie disappeared, you should open your eyes and see."

HIS NEW APARTMENT WAS a mile from mine. At night I drove by. Back. Forth. His car was there. I went into the parking lot. Scanned the cars like I would recognize which one belonged to another woman, a woman not me. I went up the cement steps. Step, step. Tiptoe quiet in my high heels. I knocked.

The door opened. Dark outside, light inside.

"Hi," I said.

"Hi," he said.

He stepped back.

I went in.

One more night of me in his bed would convince him I was the one.

We were together for those hours, me above him, me below him, me in his lap. I looked into his eyes and tried to draw out the love, like a snake charmer with a cobra, like the venom from a bite.

In the morning, when we woke, he said nothing about tomorrow, or next week, or again.

AND, LIKE MAGIC, I was gone. The girls wanted to believe. But they had to come into the other room to see if I was hiding. I ran the circle of the house, from kitchen to laundry room to bathroom to Mom and Dad's bedroom to living room to family room. Little feet behind me, Annilee behind me, Shannon behind her, not finding me.

Until they came back to the family room. And there I sat, in the same spot I'd been in when they'd closed their eyes. I had appeared again.

"Do it again," they said, both at the same time. Annilee smiling like she knew a secret, Shannon big-eyed. "Do it again."

ANOTHER YEAR WENT BY. I kept on.

His car.

Those cement steps.

Me knocking. "Can I come in?"

THIS TIME, I DISAPPEARED three times in a row, warm from running through the house, enough ahead of the girls that they never caught me. I felt magic, like I always did when I was with them.

Dad watched from his chair, smiling at his goofy daughter, his gullible granddaughters.

The girls came back to the family room, cheeks in high pink flush, sweaty wisps of hair around their foreheads. I stretched out on the floor or sat on the couch. Slowed my breath. "Wow," I said. "That last one really wore me out." They believed it was maybe true. I could make myself disappear.

"BUT WHY?" I LEANED in, over the wood table in the dining room of my apartment. "Why don't you want to be with me?" Stephen sat across from me. The one I thought was the perfect man for me.

He sat with his hands on the edge of the table. His dark eyes on me. No answer to my question.

"Why?" The pitiful, the whine and need in my voice. "What's wrong with me?" Like a mirror held up to me reflecting how Sam had tried to understand why I was leaving. Now it was me asking why of a man with no answers.

Stephen folded his arms across his chest. His shoulders curved in, protecting himself from the hurt of my words. What he had been trying to tell me all this time held in that curved hurt. Stephen wished he could love me. But it wasn't possible. Not because of me, but because of him.

I could do nothing about that.

"You have to stay away from me." I said. "Because I can't stay away from you."

Do it again. Do it again." The girls' foreheads were damp from running to find their invisible aunt.

"I have to stop," I said. "I might not be able to come back if I do it again."

We sat on the sofa, one girl on each side of me, and we took up crayons, paper. We made pictures. They drew and colored and gave their drawings to me, names in crooked child print in the corner. Annilee. Shannon. A house, a cat, a horse, a girl.

He stayed away. This man I went all out for, all in for, all over for. And I stayed away too. So that I could be done with the needing, hurting, begging, asking, trying, pleasing, longing, pleading.

So I could find answers that wouldn't have made sense to me at any other time but did right then, when everything I had been doing had stopped working.

I read self-help books that told me I was a smart woman making foolish choices who loved too much with my Cinderella complex. It all made a sad kind of sense.

Stephen's rejection burst a fence, letting loose all that I'd never let myself feel. The long trail of boys and men in my life.

What I put on them, the hope of perfection and forever falling in love, the ecstatic loss of myself. The need in me to fill up with another because it was the only way I could, for a while, feel good enough. This was the stampede that came through that fence. It wiped out the false glitter of love.

Now ANNILEE AND SHANNON are women. When I ask them did they really think I could disappear, they say, "We knew you couldn't. Not really." Do I imagine that little spark of the possible, still in their eyes? "It was fun, though," they say. "Like maybe, just maybe, you could."

ONE AFTERNOON, NEAR THE end of the time of staying away from Stephen or any other man, I walked alone to the store and bought a chocolate-covered ice cream bar. I sat on the curb and ate it in the sunshine, all by myself. *Here I am*, I thought. Here with the dark flakes of chocolate, the sweet of the ice cream, the sun on my legs.

I would take time on my own. I knew I would find another kind of love. Eventually. And I swore that when I found it, I would not fuck it up.

50. NO BELTS FOR SAFETY

I STILL LISTENED TO Bill's stories for something that would finally help me understand the absence of his desire for children. His stories still held clues.

IN HIS FATHER'S CAR, Bill and his brother are in the back seat because it's their sister's turn to have the front seat. Bill, a boy of eight, folds his arms on the back seat, rests his chin on his folded arms. Bill says, "Why did you and Mom get a divorce?"

His father tells him all the bad things about the marriage. This part Bill doesn't remember exactly, other than this inside him: *he shouldn't be telling me this.*

That wide boat of a car. No seat belts for safety.

Bill watches the road, yellow line for do not pass. "But you got us. It was all worth it, huh? Because you got us?"

Bill told me this one evening when I was digging into who his father was. Bill said, "I knew what his answer should be."

His father's arm should reach back to pat Bill's head. His father should say: *Of course, son. Of course you were worth it.* He should look at the other two children: *All three of you, are worth everything.*

But his father says, "No." His father says, "It wasn't worth it."

•

THE CLUE. THE KEY to the lock, the door swings wide.

Some wounds are too old, some decisions too long ago, some paths too harshly cut. I could not ask this man who was that boy to try to overcome. To risk us. To risk him. To risk a child.

51. ONLY FOR A PARENT

WE HAD THANKSGIVING DINNER at our house in 2000 and invited a mixed group of friends and family, including Bill's brother, Clint, and cousin Jeff and his wife Patti. Their daughter, Amber, had gone to her boyfriend's family for dinner and planned to join us for dessert.

"I can't wait for you to see her," Patti said to me. "She's so happy." That past June, Bill and Clint and I had sat next to Jeff and Patti in the audience as Amber walked the stage at her high school graduation. Her thick dark hair swung as she turned and looked toward the audience, trying find us in the crowd. We all waved.

Bill and I were proud to have been on the small invite list to be there that day with Jeff and Patti. Even though Amber wasn't more than five foot three, she looked tall in that flat board cap. "There's your girl," I'd said to Patti. She and Jeff had big grins and teary eyes. Proud and letting go at the same time.

Amber was nineteen now and had begun her first year of college. She was their only child.

Patti looked at her watch. "Maybe their dinner went late."

Bill took the pumpkin pies out of the oven. We finished washing up the dishes. Patti pulled back the cuff of her sweater and touched her watch again. She went to the kitchen window.

It was getting dark. Rain came down steadily and the street was littered with leaves. After another watch check, Patti looked at her husband and said, "She should be here by now."

I wanted Amber and her boyfriend to hurry up and get here so we could start in on the pumpkin pies while they were still warm.

"She'll be here," I said. I thought Patti worried too much about Amber. "Let's play."

We started a game of charades, and pretty soon everyone was into the loud shouts and arm waving that went with it. I forgot the time and the pies and that we were waiting for more guests.

The phone rang, and Bill stepped out of the room to get it. We kept yelling and laughing and shouting out wrong answers.

I didn't even notice when Bill came back in and gave the phone to Jeff. Bill yelled out, "Quiet," to the rest of us. Shushed us again when we didn't all stop. His eyes had turned to the glassy look he gets when something is wrong.

I went to him. "What?" I said.

He shook his head once.

Jeff listened. He said, "Okay. Okay." He hung up. "Amber was in an accident." His whole body still. "It's bad." Like giving a report. "Head injury." Holding himself back from the facts so they couldn't sink any deeper than his mouth.

Patti went down to floor, slow. Knees, hands, butt, like bones pulled down two by two. "No. No. No." Her voice rose up with each no.

I went to her, went down on my knees. Put my arms around her. "We don't know," I said. "We don't know anything yet." I helped her get her boots on.

Amber's boyfriend was driving his dad's Mustang that stormy night. The lightweight car slid and spun into the oncoming lane, right in front of a full-size van. Amber's side of the car was hit straight on. T-boned, I heard Bill tell someone later, another firefighter who knew what that meant.

Bill drove Jeff and Patti to the hospital. I helped the rest of our guests get their coats and said yes to each one when they said, "Call us when you know anything." Then Clint and I went to the hospital too. A nurse directed us to a private waiting area, a small room with two couches and two chairs and a door that shut, which meant it was serious. Patti's sister was on the way with her husband. I sat down next to Bill and across from Jeff. Bill's eyes still had that drawn-back glaze; his face was pale. I took his hand. The couches were so close that my knees brushed against Jeff's knees.

The news was bad from the start, and it didn't get any better. Pretty much the same news delivered over the hours by a nurse, a doctor, a social worker, a nurse again. Brain injury, internal bleeding. Trying to stop the bleeding inside her long enough to get her in for a brain scan to see if her brain was still alive.

After the nurse left the first time, Patti said, "If she's going to die, I want her organs donated." Preparing herself for the worst. Hours went by.

When the emergency team stopped the bleeding, they let Jeff and Patti go see Amber before they took her for the brain scan. "Do you want to come too?" Patti asked. Bill said no. I said no. It was too private. A thing only for a parent.

While they were gone, Bill and I walked out of the room, circled the bigger waiting area. People reading magazines, a big man asleep on a sofa, his hands pressed together and folded under his cheek. We didn't talk, we made that circle a few times and went back in to our little room.

When they came back, Patti said, "I don't care if she's paralyzed, I don't care if she's in a coma for the rest of her life. I want her to come home. We'll take care of her." Bargaining for better news.

The social worker said it would be hours before they knew anything. Jeff and Patti pushed us to go home. "We'll need you later," Patti said.

Bill and I hardly said a word as we drove on the wet streets, empty except for their white stripes, stoplights: yellow, red, green. It was a few hours past midnight. The rain had stopped. Tiny bits of hope, like shiny stars, drew me. That something would change in the night. The light went out of them quick. Knowing it wouldn't. The social worker, the nurse and doctors, they'd cleared the way, hour by hour taking away that hope. I asked Bill, "Is it possible she could come through this?"

"No." He came to a full stop at the corner. Only our car, the red light, the dark streets. "I talked to one of the paramedics who was on the scene." He used the turn signal. Click. Click. "Said she was brain dead." Click. Click. "The hospital has to do all this testing. So there're no questions later."

He turned onto the next street. Amber was a girl we loved, but seeing children badly injured, parents facing the first moments of grief, this wasn't new to Bill. In his job, most of the calls were medical emergencies.

He took his hand off the steering wheel and put it on my knee. These were things I relied on him for. To stay calm. To tell me the truth.

At home, we undressed and got in bed. We lay on our backs. I thought maybe I should be crying, sick to my stomach, barely able to breathe. But my breath still came.

We held hands under the covers, in and out of a haze of sleep and remembering. Each time one of us rose up from that haze, we tightened our grip.

There was this in me: It wasn't us. We didn't have to go through this. We were a step back. In the same way a woman says, "You can't know what it's like to have a child," she can say, "You can't know what it is like to lose one." I didn't want to know.

I turned on my side and looked at the outline of Bill's face. Here was the relief that we were not parents. I curled myself around it. That night, the final wanting for a child took its last steps out of me. In its absence was a hollow.

The phone rang at seven. Jeff saying to come back. They were going to take her off life support. Come say goodbye.

Amber's hospital room was full of white. White walls, white floor, white sheets, silver bed rails and heart-monitor stand. Green jagged line of her heartbeat on the black screen.

We gathered around the bed: Jeff and Patti, Patti's sister and her husband, Jeff's sister and her daughter, Bill and me, and Clint.

They'd cleaned Amber up, but flecks of dried blood were on her arm, her shoulder. She didn't look like herself. The swelling. But her dark hair, her long fingers, her mouth. These I knew. When it was my turn to say goodbye, I moved closer. I touched her hand. I wanted to say the right thing. Not for her. For Patti. For Jeff.

"I love you, Amber," I said. "Everyone's here with you." Nothing seemed right to say.

Bill was next to me. "We'll take care of your mom and dad." He cupped his hand on Amber's arm, his skin becoming the skin of an older man, hers pale and perfect.

This ending didn't seem real. Even when the nurse showed Jeff where to turn off the switch. Even when Patti nodded. Even when Amber's heart took so long to stop. That jagged line of her heart beating, beating, beating. And then slower and slower, the flat lines and long pauses between. The last one that we didn't know was the last until none came after.

The room was quiet. Jeff and Patti held each other. They were losing their only child. They were losing their family. "She's all we have," Jeff said.

A child is what makes a family. Bill and I, we were a couple. That morning, in that hospital room, with that ending, this was all I wanted us to be.

IV.
WHAT COMES WHEN
WANTING STOPS

52. MAKE A LIST

IN DECEMBER OF 1986, I made a list. The books I'd read said to ask for what you want. *Be clear, be specific, write it as if it's happening now.*

My list, bullet-pointed in a lined notebook, went something like this.

What I Want in a Man

- He is funny, has a good sense of humor.
- He is honest.
- He wants to know himself/interested in personal growth.
- He wants to know me and accepts me as I am.
- He has a good relationship with his family.
- He wants a committed relationship.
- He likes his work.
- He is healthy and fit and I like how he looks.
- He is financially secure.
- He has values that fit with mine.

It's only now, many years later, that I see what I left off the list.

I WAS TWENTY-EIGHT YEARS old, and this is what I knew: The failures of my relationships had been mostly of my own making.

I'd been a girl and become a woman who identified herself through men. Despite whatever else I did in my life, I measured my value through men. The excitement of attracting them and trying to keep them, the power of getting bored and starting the search again, recovering from leaving or being left.

A well-worn groove: in love, out of love, in love, out of love.

I didn't want to do that anymore.

But the one thing I knew I was in the world for was relationship. Connection. I'd always sought it. Not just with boys and men, but with friends with family, in the career I'd chosen. And with myself.

I wanted to be in relationship. In an ongoing, one-on-one, stay-for-the-long-term relationship, I would face myself. If I chose well. If I stayed. So far, I'd only ever stayed long enough to scratch the surface of myself.

In January a friend said to me, "There's this man I know. You might really like him. He's a firefighter, and he's really nice and easy to talk to. And he's cute."

Hope perked up in me.

"He and his wife broke up a while ago. They had a hard ending.

Wariness bumped shoulders with the hope.

"He's thirty-eight."

Reasoning stepped in. Ten years difference seemed less of big deal than when I was nineteen.

But still.

My friend said this man did a lot of the same kind of self-exploration I did. Classes and books.

"He's a really, really nice guy," she said. "Can I set you up on a date?"

Hope elbowed wariness, the way beginnings can do.

"Yes," I said.

I didn't trust myself. I could make up a whole lot of perfection in a man I didn't yet know.

But I still believed in love.

53. A WHOLE LOT OF PERFECTION

BILL CAME TO MY apartment for a double-date, blind-date, Chinese dinner date with me and my friend and her boyfriend.

I still wore my work clothes, a teal green sweater and slim black skirt and high heels, which showed off my legs and made me look pretty and professional and a little bit sexy.

Bill was tall and slim, dressed casually but also like he'd thought about it. He hugged my friend hello and shook her boyfriend's hand. The way he greeted them, said their names and looked in their eyes, made him seem like a really, really nice guy.

He shook my hand and said my name, too. Strands of curly silver hair mixed with his dark curly hair. His smile made creases around his eyes. He was handsome. A really, really handsome guy.

Immediately I went shy, and my voice went still inside me. Something about this man, this moment, all that I wanted to do differently.

We walked the few blocks to the Chinese restaurant. Bill and I ahead, my friend and her boyfriend behind. Bill had his hands in his pockets, like a really-relaxed-not-nervous guy.

"Did you just get off work?" he asked.

"Yes," I said.

"You're a counselor, right?"

"Yes," I said.

Maybe I could say something interesting about work. I looked ahead of me, looked at the ground, looked at my pumps tap-tapping the cement. The spotlight of my friend and her boyfriend right behind us, like we were on *The Dating Game* and they were the audience deciding if they should cheer this man to pick me.

The pressure of it blocked up all my words, all my thoughts.

At the Chinese restaurant, Bill and my friend talked, and sometimes the boyfriend talked. I poked my fork through the Kung Pao chicken. My friend kept looking at me with eyes that said, *Say something! Why are you so quiet?*

Mom used to say she didn't much like small talk. I guessed I shared this with her. Possible topics floated up in my head and flattened inside me. *Do you like movies? How do you like your job? What books do you like?* Everything seemed obvious and forced and small.

I wanted Bill to give me that smile again. I wanted him to Dating-Game pick me. If I could be alone with him there would be no spotlight. If I didn't know what to say, I could use my body to show him I wasn't shy.

Possibly I hadn't learned a thing about how to be different with a man.

AFTER DINNER, WE WENT back to my apartment. I must have seemed dull, and Bill must have wondered why our friend had set us up.

"Well." My friend took her boyfriend's hand. "We have to go. We, um, kind of double scheduled."

Her boyfriend looked at her with raised eyebrows. "What?"

She nudged him with her elbow and said, "Yeah, you know."

Obvious and awkward, but they left. Now was my chance.

Bill stayed near the door after they left. My date, getting

ready to pick door number two or girl number three or anyone besides me.

"Do you want something to drink?" I hoped it didn't sound too urgent or too surprising, me putting a whole sentence together.

"Sure," he said.

"Okay," I said.

I stood there.

"All I have is water or milk," I said.

"Water would be great."

I went to the kitchen and turned on the tap and ran my finger under the stream of water. *This is what I always do*, I thought. Making a man more than he is. Hoping to make him like me before I even decide if I like him. Making him so perfect and important that all my thoughts and all my words and my self dry up and float away.

The water had gone cold and I watched it run.

This is me.

But this time, I could see how I had absented myself from this man, from letting him see me or get to know me.

I filled the glass and took a long drink.

"He's just a man," I whispered. Then I filled the glass again and went back out to him.

He was leaning up against the arm of the sofa. He looked strong like a firefighter and at the same time fragile like a man who'd had some hurt. That hurt showed around his eyes and in the slimness of him. Like he hadn't always been quite as slim, like his eyes once had a little more easy trust than they did now.

I handed him the glass and sat on the couch and took a breath. The blocked-up feeling in my chest eased a little. My shoulders loosened.

He drank some water and put the glass on the coffee table and sat down near me, not too close, not too far.

"So," I said.

"So," he said.

When Mom said she didn't like small talk, she also said

she'd learned how to avoid it. *People like it when you ask questions. Plus it takes the attention off of you.*

"So," I said again. "If I were to get to know you, what would you want to tell me, and what wouldn't you want to tell me?" A twisty kind of Dating-Game question, a no-small-talk question.

He looked at me, head tipped a little to one side. Maybe my turn from mute to this one laser question had given him whiplash.

"That's a great question," he said. "I like your directness."

The watching part of me clapped her hands. He liked direct. My power.

"I have a hard time with small talk," I said. "That's probably kind of obvious. I was nervous at dinner."

"You were," he said.

My one question led to two hours of talk. Not small. What he wanted to tell me (he liked his job, he was close to his family, he tried to eat healthy, he ran, all the classes he'd taken, he liked to travel). What he didn't want to tell me (this last marriage was not his first, and the divorces felt like failures, especially the part about losing trust and feeling betrayed, he was afraid of that happening again and his health had gotten bad from the stress of it, he felt scared inside himself sometimes).

That one question led to him asking it back to me, me telling him what I wanted to tell (I was proud of where I came from, I had great fun with my nephew and nieces, I'd made a list of what I wanted in a job and got that job and really liked it, the classes I'd gone to and how they changed everything and that was part of the end of my marriage); and what I didn't want to tell (the breakup from the man I'd thought was the one and how much it hurt and I was still trying to work that out, how that man was part of the end of my marriage too, that I questioned whether I was capable of having a good relationship).

And I told what I wanted to tell (because it was always there on the tip of my tongue, the one big awful thing that had happened to me and maybe it made me seem brave and strong because I'd come through it and thought I was fine, but I'd mostly stopped speaking of because the reactions when I told were too curious or too distant), and I didn't want to tell (because maybe it would look like I needed attention from it, and maybe I did need attention, his attention, but not his pity).

"I was raped when I was twenty," I said.

The space those words make between a man and a woman. It's always there until it's told, and then it's there still.

We were facing each other. Bill had an arm propped on the back of sofa, his chin resting on his palm. He didn't say anything, but his eyes were on my eyes.

I wanted to tell more, to tell it all, to keep speaking of it until I was tired of this story.

"I'm okay," I said. Any more was too much to put on a man I'd just met. "Anyway, it was eight years ago."

He reached out and touched my shoulder. "I'm sorry that happened to you," he said. And this seemed true.

Now, WHEN PEOPLE ASK us how we met, I say, "We were a blind date." Because I like that it's kind of old fashioned and a little bit corny, and a little bit of a mystery.

Sometimes people ask, "Did you know immediately that you liked each other?"

"I liked him right off the bat," I say. I don't mention that every man I'd been with I'd liked right off the bat.

Bill says, "I wasn't that attracted to her at first. She was so quiet. And when our friends left, I thought, 'Well this will be interesting, I wonder if this woman will have anything to say.' But then we were alone, and she was real and direct and curious. That's when I saw she was pretty too."

It was with Bill that I learned that what is inside me animates me, and this gives me beauty.

I TOLD HIM HOW I'd made a list of what I wanted in a man.

"What was on that list?" he asked.

After I went through what was on the list, he said, "Mine

would be pretty close to that. What I'd want in a woman. Honesty would be a big thing on it. Honesty and trust."

Honesty and trust. Didn't everyone want those things? I'd always thought I did. But I was beginning to understand it was hard to be honest with someone else if you weren't being that way with yourself. And if you weren't honest with yourself, how did you even know?

Eventually, he looked at his watch. "The time went fast," he said. "I should be going."

He stood up and I stood up, thinking maybe this is the part where he wants to do more than talk. Because this is what I always did, moved past the talking.

"Can I give you a hug?" he asked.

A hug.

"Yes," I said.

It was an arms-around-me, straight-on hug. And then he stepped back. He had a scar on his upper lip, faded and thin.

"I don't quite know what it is about you," he said. "But I really want to see you again. We seem to want the same things in life."

I felt off kilter and a little bit proud. We met, we talked, we hugged goodnight. A proper date.

I went to the window and watched him go out to his car. The tall, slim, back of him, that head of curly hair, the way he held his shoulders curved in a little. Two marriages, he'd said. That was a lot of marrying and divorcing for a man not quite forty. But who was I to speak, with the long line behind me? I was beginning to regard that line, all those boys and men, not as failures, but as research.

54. MAYBE A LOVE SOUND, MAYBE A HEARTBREAK

BILL'S CAR LOOKED LIKE a shiny black beetle, and on our second date, I didn't have to search for small talk. "Cool car," I said, when he picked me up.

It had been a week since our first date, and I'd spent plenty of time thinking about him. Playing out the words we'd said, his smile, that scar on his upper lip, his dark eyes on me. I felt hopeful, and scared at how hopeful I felt.

I'd mentioned to a friend that I had a date with Bill. This friend had met him before. Her lips went in a downward direction and she crinkled her nose. "He might be kind of boring for you," she said. She thought I liked wild men.

I'd mentioned him to another friend who had met Bill before. The lines between his eyebrows deepened. "I don't know if he's for you," he said. "I think he likes to party." He thought I liked calm men.

People putting stories on other people.

Now here Bill was picking me up at my apartment, opening the car door for me. Another proper date, dinner date, I-hope-I-have-something-interesting-to-say date. I had on a silky blouse, another slim skirt, heels. I tucked my stockinged calves, one, two, into the car and he shut the door. He walked to his side of the car, his long, lean body passing in front of me, his shoulders with that small inward curve, the angle of his cheekbones. I was not bored.

He turned the engine on, a purr and rumble.

"What kind of car is this?" In my head: *What kind of man are you?*

"It's a Saab." He pulled out onto the road, shifted up, and up again.

"I like it." In my head: *I like you.*

The purry engine sound deepened as he accelerated. "Me too," he said. About the car, not about what he couldn't hear, the chattering inside me.

Some bubbly no-words music played on the stereo. He turned it up. A bubbly no-words warmth moved from my ears to my throat, down my chest, into my stomach.

I wanted to sway with the music, put my hand on his thigh, feel the vibration of the engine, feel his muscles move with the acceleration. Feel the possibility of him.

I looked out the window at the dark shadows of firs and cedars, the prism of streetlights. I took a breath. In my head: *Slow down. Slow down.*

"I bought this car in Sweden," he said into the space of my quiet. He shifted from third to fourth, fourth to fifth. He'd picked the car up and then driven it for five weeks all over Europe, then had it shipped home. "I actually saved money that way."

"Wow," I said. "Five weeks in Europe?"

We were on the freeway, heading toward downtown, red taillights of other cars ahead.

"It was our honeymoon," he said.

Record needle stop on my heart, that bubbly music not in my ears anymore. How had he said it? *Honeymoon.* Maybe with an achy sound. Maybe a love sound, wishing and romance. Maybe a heartbreak.

I could've put a check mark next to "financially stable" on my list of things I wanted in a man, been impressed with him putting together a trip to Europe with buying a car. I could've been happy he kept the car and not the wife.

"How long ago was that?" I said.

"Europe?" he said. "About two years ago."

Somehow, in that talk on the couch, I'd missed these fine details.

"Have you traveled a lot?" In my head: *Are you done with that marriage? And how exactly long has it been since you split up? And why did you split up, and what did she do wrong in only two years?* It didn't occur to me to wonder what he might have done wrong.

The questions bunched up in my throat. We were only on a second date. I would sound like a jealous woman, a nosy woman nosing in.

When I'd been with Stephen, the man I thought was the one, I searched for his secrets when he was away, put my hands in the pockets of empty coats, read letters tucked on shelves, opened desk drawers, fanned books for notes and secrets. Evidence to understand why I was not enough.

"I love to travel," Bill said.

"What places have you gone to?" I asked.

Stephen had noticed. A letter moved here, a note put back on the wrong page, the worry-scent of me lingering in pockets and drawers.

Bill listed the places he'd been. "Well, all over Europe. I've been to Canada," he said. "New York, New Orleans. My favorite is the desert southwest. Oh, and Mexico. My ex-wife got me traveling to Mexico. I love it there."

How did he say that? Wife. Ex. Did he love her still? Had she broken his heart? Was he done?

My worry-chatter exhausted me. But Bill spoke of his past matter-of-factly, no love or heartbreak in sight.

"How about you?" he asked.

"Me, what?"

Stephen had confronted me. *Have you been reading my letters? Looking at my things?*

No, I'd lied.

"Have you traveled?" Bill asked me now. "Do you like to travel?"

At first I thought to say yes. But that wasn't true. I didn't want to start with hiding. "I don't know," I said. "I feel kind of embarrassed that I've hardly been anywhere. Just around Oregon and Washington. A little bit of California. And Montana." Things I'd done with other men, and why should this be a secret? "I like the Oregon coast. That's where my ex-husband and I went for our honeymoon."

Here I began a new kind of searching. Catching myself hiding when there was no reason to hide other than some tangled idea that love didn't exist without jealousy.

WHITE TABLECLOTHS AND CANDLELIGHT, my grilled prawns and his red snapper. Bill leaned in toward me.

"You grew up on a ranch?"

I nodded. "I grew up in the house my great-grandfather homesteaded. My dad has lived in that same house all his life." I never tired of telling this, the long legacy of home always with me. "I lived in the same house until I was eighteen," I said. "Same house, same school, same town."

In this restaurant that Bill had found when he asked a friend for a special place, the spotlight of him warmed me.

"I have no idea what that would be like," he said. "We moved thirteen times by the time I was through high school."

All that moving. I took a few bites. In my grade school a new crop of kids cycled through each year. They only stayed for one year and then they were gone. They lived at the airbase outside of town, children of air force parents. Those kids had been to Germany and Japan and, for show-and-tell, they brought foreign coins and coconuts made into masks and elephants carved from alabaster. I brought the stuffed dog I'd gotten at Christmas and once a three-legged salamander I'd caught in the creek. But even if those students had exotic things for show-and-tell, they kept to the sidelines at recess, got picked last for the softball games.

They tried to fit in with us Condon kids, but our roots were like arms locked one to another in a birthright game of Red Rover. I couldn't imagine moving thirteen times.

"My father left when I was one," Bill said. "Mom didn't have much money. We had to move a lot." His voice, his words, didn't sound like he felt sorry for himself. But in the telling we discovered the important differences between us.

It would take us years to understand what these differences meant. When I was a kid, for a big change Mom moved sofas and tables and rearranged the arrangements. Us kids swapped bedrooms. I took the yellow room, Leanne took the green room, Pat took over the bunkhouse, Brad got the big bedroom all to himself. Same house, new look.

The first time Bill was out of town, a year after we moved in together, I decided to rearrange the furniture. My big surprise. He came home to the sofa and bookshelves and framed pictures all in new places. He stood in the doorway. Still body. Eyes blinking. He could hardly speak. He wasn't angry, he was lost. His mother always kept things the same, as much as she could, in each new house. Sofa in front of the picture window, bed always facing the same direction. The same ornaments on a white flocked tree, year after year. New house, same look. She would tuck Bill and his brother in at night: *Here is your bed, here is your pillow, here is your blanket, here I am. Everything the same.*

55. THE TURN TO MY HOUSE

AFTER DINNER AND A walk, we got back in the Saab and drove toward my place. That music was still on the stereo. "Deep Breakfast," Bill said. He turned up the volume. "It's my favorite right now." Bubbles and violins filled the car. He rested his hand on the brake lever, right next to my leg.

"I like it." I'd mostly forgotten about the honeymoon, how recent his marriage, how short. "It sounds happy."

He missed the turn that would have put us on the freeway back to my apartment. "The guy plays all the instruments." Bill turned the music down a little. "He makes one sound and then dubs over with the next and the next." He turned left.

"What other kind of music do you like besides this?" I asked.

"Janis Joplin. Elton John. The Moody Blues," he said. "Oh, Rod Stewart. I really like him." He turned right. "What kind of music do you like?" He asked.

"Talking Heads," I said. "Prince."

"I don't really know their music," he said. Soon we would make this a challenge, introducing each other to things we didn't know because of the ten years between us.

He made more turns, going on streets in the wrong direction from home. Maybe he was taking me to his house. Maybe I wanted to go to his house.

"Oh and Cat Stevens," I said. "I've liked his music forever."

"Have you ever been to the top of Council Crest?"

"No," I said. "I think I've heard of it." Maybe it was a make-out place.

"It's the highest point in Portland. Great view."

For sure we were going to park, like I hadn't done since college. I breathed in, to see if my breath smelled of prawns and garlic.

"I really like Cat Stevens, too," Bill said.

Car lights shone in behind us and framed the curve of curly hair at the back of his head. I liked how he looked. Dark eyes and eyebrows, strong nose.

I wanted to know everything. I started with an easy question. "Do you have kids?" The automatic question for anyone who is married or has been married, even though anyone with kids would have already mentioned he had kids.

"No," he said. "No kids."

Another left, another right. It didn't seem like we were going uphill at all.

How could a man have two marriages and almost thirty-nine years and not have kids? I tried to think of any man his age I knew who didn't. But the absence of children came as a relief. I'd already stepped into my hopes for our future and I didn't want it to include the child negotiation with another wife.

He slowed, pulled over to the side of the road and put the car in neutral. He turned and looked out his window, in one direction, then the other.

"I have to tell you something," he said.

In my head: *Uh-oh.*

"I missed the turn to get on the freeway to your place and tried to cover it up by saying I'd take you to Council Crest. Now I must've missed the turn to get there."

He got lost. He told me. This made me like him even more.

He put the car in gear and turned back the way we'd come. He smiled into the light of the console. "I think I got nervous." His voice had a surprise to it. He looked over at me. "I think it's being with you." He put his hand on my knee, light and easy. "A good kind of nervous."

He kept his eyes on the road. His profile looked familiar already. I didn't know yet how often I would be here next to him, that I would always love looking at him this way.

"Anyway, about your question," he said. "My mom always says we raised each other, and that's kind of true. I was responsible from a young age. Didn't really get to be a kid. Maybe that's why I never really wanted any of my own." The engine purred; the heater blew warm air on my feet. This moment felt intimate. "Now, so much time has gone by. I'm almost forty. I don't want to be an older dad."

"I used to think I'd have kids," I said. "My ex-husband and I were trying before we split up." And there, in the comfort of that car, the awareness that had come to me in those classes went from maybe to surety. "I started to think about why I wanted to have children, other than it's just what's expected. There are already so many kids in the world."

With Bill next to me, the possibility of this other kind of life seemed solid. "Now I don't think I want kids."

I believed this then. He believed it.

Maybe it was true. It felt true, the letting go of legacy and expectation. Or maybe my old habits held strong, and I was lining myself up to be a perfect match.

One song ended and another started, and before I'd gotten used to his hand on my knee, he moved it and turned up the dial on the stereo. "I love this song." Then he laughed and said, "I put this tape on and cued up that first song when I got to your apartment so it would start playing when I turned on the stereo. Trying to impress you."

This new song had violin sounds that I felt in my belly and chest, like a longing, like love, like both at the same time.

"I think I got nervous too," I said. "When I realized you were married just two years ago and already it didn't work. Are you sure you're done with it?"

"I'm sure," he said. He kept his eyes on the road. "We were already together three years before that. She was sad a lot and I kept trying to make her happy. She wanted a house and we built a house. Then she said she'd be happy if we could be married. So we got married. But that didn't help. Then she wanted a baby. I didn't think a child would make her feel better or fix things between us."

"Oh," I said. Maybe this was what had gone wrong in the marriage. She wanted a child too much. Maybe this was what he'd done wrong. Didn't want a child enough.

He said, "I've had two divorces." He looked at me, then back at the road. "I want to be careful. Make sure I'm with someone who is okay in her own self." He meant me. He meant he needed to be careful with me. "I want to be sure I'm with someone who doesn't make me responsible for her happiness."

"Okay," I said. I folded my hands together. Clasped them tight.

I felt shaky and scared. I was pretty sure I'd been doing that all this time, with all the men I'd been with. Looking for someone to make me happy. I always felt happy with them at first. And then I didn't.

It would take me a few years to see that story went both ways. Bill had his part. He'd been taking responsibility for the happiness of the women in his life. A responsibility that wasn't his to take.

The music switched to another song, pretty and sad, with an ache of long held-out notes and spaces in between.

56. LANGUAGE I COULD SPEAK SO EASILY

THE DOOR TO BILL'S house had a rectangle of opaque glass, and the light that came through was gold. I touched my hair, pressed my lipstick lips together. After three weeks and four dates, I was at his house. Finally a not-out-in-public date.

I rang the doorbell. Inside, the shadow of Bill moved toward me. The door opened and there he was. Curls, shoulders, slim hips, long legs, him.

"You're here," he said. He pulled the door wide.

"I'm here." Our fourth date, and I'd be completely alone with him in a we-can-do-anything kind of way.

I stepped up the step into his house, my heels *tap tap* on the entry floor. He hugged me. Three dates so far and nothing more than a hug. I wanted more. I wanted to put my lips to his ear, to whisper: *Please, move your hands lower. Lower still. Yes. There. Pull me to you.*

He stepped back. The lamplights in the front room were set low; two tall plants in wicker baskets columned either side of the sofa. One was a palm, and the other looked like something from a jungle, with wide curving leaves and rough textured bark.

The rust-orange brushed-velvet sofa had many pillows. I wanted to stop there, fall on it with bare skin, pull the length of his body on mine. Whisper: *Please, could we finally be together this way? It's coming on a month of knowing you and I won't really know you until I know you with my clothes off.*

He led me through the living room, into the bright-light kitchen. More plants at the windowsill, heart-shaped leaves in dark green and light green trailed the length of it. A wok on the cooktop, chopped vegetables and shelled prawns on a cutting board. The kitchen was open to a family room with a wood stove, a TV, two more tall plants, a sectional sofa in a nubby beige. *We could start here. Let's skip your nice dinner and go for the dessert of skin on skin.*

He turned the burner on under the wok. "I'm making stir-fry," he said. "I know you like prawns." He remembered.

We chatted about my day, his day. I walked around the family room. Touched the arm of the nubby sofa. He had a wood stove. He had a stereo. He had end tables. He had a wok. I looked out the window and myself reflected in the dark. I was slim, my dark hair perm-curly, chin length. My nose that my first boyfriend said was too big. I didn't know if I was pretty enough. Maybe all Bill wanted was a friend.

"Your house is really nice," I said. His grown-up house. His grown-up life. I wanted to be grown-up with him. But first: *Let's be like teenagers, let's jump in the sack, let's get it done.*

"Thanks," he said. "But I can't take all the credit for it. My ex-wife did a lot of it."

I took a quick breath in. I'd had a talk with myself to remember that this is what he did. He spoke of her as someone who had been in his life.

"She has good taste," I said.

He'd said he was done with her. But still. Why was this house so complete? Why did he get to keep it all? Would she come back for more? Were they really done?

"She left you with most of it?" I couldn't help myself.

"She moved to a small apartment and got some new furniture. She took a lot of the nice things." He said it without blame or complaint.

"Well, it looks great anyway," I said.

"She agonized over it, to make it this way. Each thing. She cared too much about having it be perfect."

I would be different. I didn't need everything perfect. Forgetting the memory of my ex-husband's worried eyes when he found me on my hands and knees scrubbing invisible grime from the corners of the bathroom in the townhouse we moved to after the rape. Dust and dirt, dirt and dust, dark in corners. Like fingerprint powder. The crime scene that followed us from one apartment to the next, to the next. When Sam had found me there with a toothbrush and bucket of hot soapy water, he said "What are you doing?" Like it was a crime to want perfection. "Cleaning," I said. "It's dirty, I'm cleaning."

Bill stirred onion and garlic in hot oil. He added the carrots. Steam rose around him.

"I had a Christmas cactus once." I pointed at the one in the window, blooming pink blooms. "But I watered it too much." I could show him all the ways I could be perfectly imperfect.

"Yes, I guess they don't like much water," Bill said. He put in the zucchini, the mushrooms. He stirred the stir-fry.

I still had an African violet from my grandmother. It sometimes bloomed dark purple blooms. African violets like damp soil.

"You must have a green thumb," I said.

I still had a plant from a start given to me by the mother of a boy I'd dated in high school. Long spear leaves, with creamy stripes running through a green so dark it was almost black. Mother-in-law's tongue, she'd called it when she handed me the starts, the ends wrapped in damp paper towel, her smile sweet like an inside joke.

"No," Bill said, "I'm not sure what I'm doing at all. I'm lucky they're alive. My ex couldn't fit them in her apartment."

On one shelf was a terra-cotta figure, about a foot tall, a

man hunched over carrying a kind of basket on his back. I went to it.

"I found that in Mexico," Bill said. "She didn't like it." He didn't sound bitter, maybe a little sad. "But I bought it anyway. I put it out after she moved."

I touched the rough sand skin of the terra-cotta man, cool under my fingers. Could he see I loved it too, this man with the burden on his back?

Bill picked up the bowl of prawns and tipped them into the wok. More steam, the low hiss and murmur of vegetables mixing with heat and the prawns turned from pale pink to pale white and the heat reached me. *Put that spoon down, turn the burner off, let's eat later.*

He turned down the heat, spooned the food to the waiting plates, and I followed him into the dining room. We sat knees-touching close.

Dinner was delicious. My favorite kind of food, like he already knew, vegetables and rice and prawns. I hardly ate five bites. My appetite was taken by the wanting whispers of my body.

"I rented a movie," he said. "*Short Circuit*. A friend recommended it."

I'd heard of that movie. Something about a robot and maybe for kids. It didn't matter. We would sit on that big nubby sofa in the room with the TV.

Bill put the tape in the VCR. He sat next to me, his leg along my leg, his shoulder touching my shoulder.

The movie started. I slipped my pumps off, tucked my legs under me, and leaned closer. He put his arm around me. He smelled of heat and musk cologne. He pulled me closer. I liked it there.

Fifteen minutes in, he said, "This is kind of a kids' movie, isn't it?" Maybe his friend was having a joke on him.

"Yes, I guess it is." My face was close to his and his was close to mine. This became a kiss that became something else, like fluid and ease. He stretched out and pulled me to him. In that fluid move the two of us were the length of each other. I moved on top of him. He ran his hands down my back, my waist, to lower and he pulled me closer. I pressed into him. He put his hand under my skirt, moved it up my thigh. Up to the top of my stocking. Bare skin, strap of garter belt, panties. What I wanted to share with him.

"Wow," he said.

All thought went away, and this was all we said for a long time. Bit by bit we left our clothes behind. We went, slow and urgent, from here (the couch) to there (his bed).

AFTER THE FAMILIAR RELIEF and pleasure, the unthinking-only-feeling discovery of someone new, we looked once more at each other.

Bill said it again. "Wow."

And I smiled and said, "Yeah. Wow."

The relief of this part finally being done. The worry of how familiar it felt, the glittery firstness of it. What I hoped wouldn't go away when I knew him more, when he knew me more.

I'd been here before. But this was the longest I'd ever gone from knowing someone to sleeping with him.

He laughed, "I can't believe that happened."

"You can't?" Because it did and why wouldn't it and what was unbelievable about it? "What do you mean?"

He pulled me close. His hands were warm, gliding over my back. I felt like silk.

"Oh, I had this plan," he said. "It's kind of silly when I think about it." He smoothed his hand, down my arm, my thigh. "I wanted to wait and be friends first. Before. You know. This."

Did I hear disappointment in the space between the words? He hadn't seemed disappointed when he was inside me, kissing me, moving with me.

"Really?" I said. I propped myself up on my elbow, pulled the sheet up over my nakedness. I was cold. I looked around the room. I'd never done this with a friend. Why would I want to miss out on this part? The fast and new. The unknown. The surprise of me showing him how bold, how easy, how free I could be. This place where we didn't have to speak, just do what our bodies wanted.

The bed had no headboard; the comforter, now thrown to the foot of the bed, was faded. She had cleared all the beauty from this room.

"I have this feeling," he said. "About you. We could have something really special. I thought if I waited, if we went really slow, if I really got to know you as a friend. Like six months or something, I'd be doing something different. Break a pattern. And we'd have something really intimate, being friends first."

How would we have gone from friends to this? I tried to imagine it and felt only a dull feeling in me. As far as I knew, it only worked this way. When the friend part happens, this breathless part changes. To something too familiar.

It didn't occur to me that this idea of friends first could have worked too, could have been the something different that would mean I didn't fuck this up. I didn't trust friendship yet. I only trusted what my body could do.

I stretched alongside him, moved my hand down, touched him. This man scared me. He wanted to know me. "You should have told me," I said.

He moved to the rhythm of my hand. "I was crazy to think I could wait." He pulled me to him like our bodies could melt together. "I'm glad we didn't."

He wasn't disappointed. But in his holding, his touch, in his house, this bare bedroom, it was possible I scared him too. The possibility of what could happen if we weren't careful.

He ran his hands down my back. "You are beautiful," he said. It was the first time he'd said anything like this. Over the years he would tell me this when he touched me.

With Bill, beauty is a felt thing. One of a thousand ways we would find we were different. Him tactile, me visual. Him thinking we could wait, me not. Him wanting intimacy, me thinking that's what this was, us here in bed, too guarded to have ever known anything else, to speak what was inside of me, to even know it myself.

IN THE MORNING, WHEN I left early to go home and get ready for work, Bill held me in a long hug; his hands went down my back, low, and pulled me to him. We made plans to see each other that night.

"I'm glad we didn't wait," he said.

I pressed myself into him. This language I could speak so easily.

On my way out, I went past the sculpture of the man bent forward by the burden on his back. Jorge, we would start calling him. He would always be in our home.

I went out through that front room, those tall plants in their wicker baskets. For the first years after I moved into Bill's house, I would try to keep these tall plants alive because I thought they were his too, not just hers. The leaves of the palm yellowed, they curled and dropped; the jungle plant sent out a single glorious bloom, and I thought I'd made a miracle until Mom told me some plants bloom when they are stressed. A few months later the trunk of the jungle plant, with its rough bark, thinned and melted. All of his ex-wife's plants died. Even the Christmas cactus.

When one died, I bought another to replace it, thinking Bill wanted tall tropical plants in his home. Until finally I stopped. I said, "You know, these plants are a lot of work. And I don't know how to keep them alive." He said, "I don't care, they aren't my thing. I thought you wanted them."

My mother-in-law's tongue lived. The African violet lived, and I divided it once and again. I bought two hardy lipstick plants, and Mom gave me a start of her hoya plant that blooms once in a while, small waxy flowers each with a single drop of nectar, like a teardrop. These plants don't mind being root-bound, they like less attention, not more, and I have kept them alive.

57. DAYS OF EASY FALLING

SMALL YELLOW NOTES FROM me, left on the bathroom mirror in the morning:

I love you.

I'll miss you today.

Small yellow notes from him, left on the counter in the morning:

You are special.

I've never been this happy.

Thank you for last night.

A phone call in the middle of the workday in the second month of us. "I was driving along, and all of a sudden I noticed how green everything is," Bill said. It was early spring, and the new green of the Willamette Valley was particularly dazzling when the sun shone. "But more green than usual," he said. "Like I was really, really, seeing it. Because of falling in love."

I looked at the pale green buds on the rhodies that hinted of the pink blooms to come. At the new grass in front of the building. And the blue sky so blue.

"Me too," I said.

Green became our word for these days of easy falling.

We both knew this was the falling, not the staying.

In bed at night, talking and touching after making love,

we learned each other, the paths to our hurts, the paths to our strengths. The trampoline scar on his lip, the mill-accident scar on his elbow. The barbed-wire scar on my thigh, the iron burn on my forearm.

We spoke of our hidden scars, the one on his heart from betrayal, the one on mine from rejection. My fear of open closet doors, the memory of a stranger with a knife; Bill's missing of a distant father, weariness from women he couldn't fix but thought he should be able to. I shared as much as I knew about myself in that moment, and he shared as much as knew about himself.

This was the starting place. This was the skin, and what was below the skin. We didn't yet know our subterranean, our hidden. We would discover this together. We'd each had our own experiences, past loves. We now knew it is with the other that we learn about ourselves. The mirrors we hold up.

For now, everything was green, and we were like the ant from the fable, storing love away for the winter we both knew would come: the inevitable struggle for power and love and self that had spelled the end of each of our past relationships. This spring of ours would turn, too, the struggle would come, and we would make our own story, we would make our own scars.

WHEN BILL LEFT ME alone in his house the first time, there were cupboards and closets and drawers to search. The hunt for clues that could hurt me. Old habits.

One ear listened for his return. Two hands opened an album in the hall closet, pictures of his first wedding. Him in a pale-yellow suit, his curls combed straight. His head was turned and tilted down to her; she was tall and lean and tan, her hand on his arm. She looked like a city girl, with long hair parted down the middle and eyes that said, "He is mine." She was prettier than me. This picture couldn't tell me what went wrong.

In a tin on his dresser I found an on old badge from the fire department. I held the weight of it in my palm. I liked that he was a fireman. He said his job wasn't that dangerous. Most of the calls they went on were medical. Little kids, young people hurt or dying. A different kind of danger.

He'd told me that being a firefighter hadn't been a childhood dream or a young man's ambition. He came across the job by accident, a neighbor by a mailbox on a Wednesday afternoon. A neighbor who said this is a job where you work twenty-four hours on, forty-eight hours off. To a young man like Bill, this sounded like the ideal job to give him freedom.

I found a shoebox filled with small pieces of colored paper, each in a different handwriting, each addressed to him.

You are one of the kindest men I know.

Remember self-compassion.

Thank you for being there when I needed you.

You are a warm and loving man.

Your honesty blows me away.

I knew these kinds of notes, notes that people wrote to each when they took the sort of classes I'd taken back in Eugene. This was part of what drew me to Bill. He'd taken even more classes than I had.

The closet and drawers held nothing to hurt me, only clues to who he was.

He had told me about that book, *The Magic of Believing*, that he'd ordered off an advertisement at the back of a magazine. I loved that boy who'd already been searching. I loved this man who kept all these notes to remind himself that he was good.

THINGS COULD GO WRONG. To protect myself, I'd ask, "When you say you love me, what does that mean?" Rather than saying what I wanted: *I want it to be only you and me.* Three months together was long enough to know.

For Bill, the question was just the question, and he answered it exactly. "It means I love you." He never looked behind the question for the hidden doors, the indirect way I'd learned growing up to ask for what I wanted without risking myself.

I took another arcing shot. "Does that mean we're not seeing other people?"

"Of course," he said, a why-do-you-even-need-to-ask surprise in his voice. "I want it to be you and me. Exclusive."

This was not enough. "We don't sleep with anyone else, right? And we don't date anyone else, right?" Setting the rules with my questions so it looked like him setting the rules. If he got the answers right.

"Yes," he said. And, "Oh, there's one thing." Like he just remembered. "There's a woman I was dating before I met you. She likes to go out dancing, and I still want to do that once in a while."

"Dancing?" I kicked that word like barbed wire was wrapped around it. Dancing was touch. Dancing was sexy. Dancing led to other things.

"You don't really like to dance," he said.

A week after we'd made love that first time, we'd gone to a club with strobe lights and a steady techno beat and songs I didn't know. Even though in those seminars I'd learned to love dancing, my old shyness had returned. I might not find the beat, feel the music, look good enough and free enough for him to keep liking me. I stayed in my chair.

Lost on me then was the fact that I could fall into bed with him more easily than I could dance in front of him.

"Next song," I'd said. Then, "No, not this one, maybe next."

I couldn't keep saying no.

Finally, we went to the dance floor. I moved a few stiff steps, then a few more. He wasn't watching. I moved again, easy, easier, felt the steady rhythm in my feet, in my legs, my body. My arms opened wide, I closed my eyes, remembering: *Oh yeah, I love to dance.* And when I was almost lost in the music, I opened my eyes.

He was dancing, happy, like that fizzy bubbly music on his stereo. He did not hold the beat. He was like a boy. Bouncing. He smiled at me. I looked around to see if anyone saw him not holding the beat, looking the way he looked. My laugh was not a this-is-fun laugh, but a nervous settle-down-you-look-silly laugh. My hands went to his arms, to slow him down, to make him look sexier, to make it look like I wanted to be closer. I slipped my hands into his and tried to lead him in the swing, but he flung me too far. He let go and started to dance alone again. I lost the beat, I stopped moving. "I'm sorry," I said. "Sometimes I feel like dancing, and sometimes I don't."

We left the bar not long after. We hadn't gone dancing again.

I didn't want to dance with him. I didn't want him to dance with another woman. I corralled him with my jealous questions. "Where's the line? How do you know she knows that's all it is? What if she thinks it's something more? What if you really like dancing with her and one thing leads to another?" In each question was the demand, the command: *You can't dance with her.*

"What if I asked you all those questions about going to a movie with your ex-boyfriend? I trust that you know the line and you've been clear with him about it," he said.

"That's different." Me and Stephen, the man I had thought was the one. A dark theater. Arms, shoulders, legs, close. "It's just." I stopped talking. That man and I had already been something more than dance partners. We were going backward now and becoming friends. No sex, no possible sex. I trusted myself almost completely.

I folded my arms. "I don't want you to dance with her."

"You're trying to control me." Bill's voice was quiet and patient.

I wanted the magic power of my silence to twist his arms, to get him to give in, to say he wouldn't dance with her.

"You can't control me with jealousy," he said. "With not talking. I see it. It won't work." He would say this and what followed again over the years, until I finally understood. "I love you. You can trust me. But this is your thing to work through."

He called out my old familiar tricks. He set them between us, as though holding up a mirror with a you-can-do-this-another-way sureness. My ugly fears were reflected.

The image sent me scrambling backward. The girl I'd always been scrambling and flailing at a cliff, like the cartoon coyote with nothing to grab on to.

Except this.

"I trust you," he said. "I want you to trust me."

This is when I began to understand that jealousy is not love, and angry silence doesn't change a thing; they were weapons aimed at my own heart.

"Okay," I said. Swallowing, breathing. "Okay." Hitting the ground, not broken, but someplace completely new.

Over the years I would teach him the Western Swing. He would dance it with me, badly at first, swing me out too far or with not enough sureness in his arms. I told him the moves. "Spin me. Hand behind your back. Wring the washrag." I'd grab his hand and twirl myself. We would keep dancing, wherever there was music. One day, we would go out on a dance floor and he'd swing me just the right distance, his arms strong and loose. When I reached for his hand before he offered it to me, he would say, "Let me lead." And I would.

He never did go dancing with that dancer.

"How do you know you're loved?" I asked him.

"The notes you leave me, the way you touch me."

"How do you know you're loved?" he asked me.

"Flowers are one way. Plus, when you tell me."

An any-day-no-special-reason bouquet of carnations, dyed pale green and pink and blue, was delivered to me at work. The card said, *"Everything is still so green."*

We had made it through that talk a month earlier, and we were still falling in love.

"Thank you for the flowers." Phone in one hand, cupping one pale blue bloom with the other. "They're pretty. Carnations." I'd never really liked carnations before; Mom always said they were a cheap flower.

"I love carnations," he said. "They last a long time."

The simplicity of these flowers. The complete lack of pretension in this man. Nothing underneath, nothing to read into or look for. No guessing. I learned and admired this about him, but it would take years for me to really trust that he meant what he said.

I was beginning to see that I kept things hidden and expected to be guessed at. Wrong answer and we all lose. With this man, I wanted to come out from hiding.

HE ASKED ME TO help him pick out a new bed. "I want you to like it too," he said. We'd been together five months, and I spent most nights at his house. I helped him choose, Danish modern blond and sleek, with matching dressers, one long and low, one tall and narrow.

In the mornings, when neither of us had to work, we stayed there. This one room in the house was more him than her.

"I love your new furniture." I ran my hand across the cool grain of the wood.

"Every time I look at it, I feel guilty," he said. His voice sounded worn down by the weight of this gift to himself.

"Why?" I put my hand on his chest.

"My mom's never had anything this nice. I feel bad. Spending money on it when I could do something for her."

"Wow," I said. "I look at it and think you have something beautiful that you worked hard for."

"I look at it and feel like I don't deserve it," he said.

This is when I knew he was broken in his own ways, and that I was strong in my own ways.

"You take on burdens that no one asks you to take on." I would say this many times over the years. "You can't give love without giving to yourself," I said. "I want you to love this bed." I moved his hand to my breast. "I love being here with you."

And we took in another kind of beautiful.

"How DO YOU SHOW your love?" I asked him.

"Honesty. I tell you what's going on for me. And I touch you."

"How do you show your love?" he asked me.

"I tell you. I look for what's important to you and try to give that back."

58. HOW EASILY
I COULD HURT

AT A MOVIE, BILL watched me. I saw him out the corner of my eye. Over and over he looked away from the screen, his eyes on my face. I ate popcorn, laughed at the lines, and pretended I didn't see him watching me. Enchanted. Captivated. Even after five months together, he thought I was better than what was on the screen.

After the movie, I waited for him to take my hand, take me in his arms, tell me how much he loved me. He didn't do any of that. He said. "I had the weirdest feeling. A really strong urge to go home and be alone. Put the stereo on and turn the music up and be by myself."

"Oh." I was a falling heart. He wasn't enchanted. Not captivated by me throwing wads of popcorn into my wide-open mouth and laughing my silly laugh.

"Okay." I held my don't-let-him-see-you-hurt face, like a thousand tiny bricks building back the wall I'd let down over these months.

"Listen to me." He bent a little at his knees to catch my eyes. "It's not what you think. That's why I'm telling you."

He said, "I was watching you and I felt all this love for you.

Huge. It was overwhelming, because I realized you could go away. I wanted to protect myself. To be alone. I'm telling you now so you know me. So you'll know how I feel about you."

To know himself this well. To reveal himself this way. This stunned me and scared me.

"I don't even like to listen to the stereo by myself," he said.

The small tremble in his cheeks.

How easily I could hurt him.

ON A WEEKEND TRIP to the ocean Bill and I walked on the beach, held hands. The waves moved in and out, a fog bank hovered on the horizon. I stopped and picked up a small white rock.

"Here," I said. I turned to Bill and placed the rock in his palm. "Keep this to remember this day and how much I love you." He smiled and kissed me and put the small rock in his pocket.

We walked on a little farther and he let go of my hand. "I'll catch up," he said. I kept walking, imagining he was looking at me, admiring me from behind.

"Jackie," he called out. Then louder. "Jackie." His voice was strained.

I turned. He had a huge rock in his hands, heavy enough to hunch him over. He pretend-staggered toward me. "Here," he said. "I want you to keep this to remember this day and how much I love you." This man made me laugh.

ONE NIGHT, AFTER MANY months of mornings and afternoons and evenings of making love, I didn't come. After, when Bill was on his back and I had my head on his shoulder, and his breath was smooth and mine was the same as it had been because this time it hadn't gone fast, he didn't ask me why I didn't come or what he had done wrong. I wouldn't have had an answer anyway. I was used to this pattern. Sex was easy with a man, until we got to know each other. Until it was safe and he loved me.

Bill said, "I'll do what you like if you tell me and show me." He reminded me, my body was my own. "But you're responsible for your orgasm. And I'm in charge of mine."

No man had ever said a thing like this.

Alone, I'd understood this. The pleasure I could give myself. But, with a man, I didn't know how. My focus always on him, his needs, his pleasure.

"Okay," I said. "I'll let you know if there is anything." I turned on my side, away from him and spooned my back into his front. I pretended to be tired.

This talk made me feel bare, exposed. I didn't know what to say. I didn't know what I liked or didn't like when I was with a man.

I'd been on a long search for the man who would find the magic way of me, how I could make myself feel when I was alone. At first, with each boy or man, I thought I'd found it. But the pleasure of my body came from the paperback-novel excitement of first times and the unknown, of imagining our perfection. The excitement of showing off: *See how sexy and free I am! See how easy it is for me!*

After a month, or months, or a year, the heat of the new cooled, and it wasn't easy anymore.

Maybe this was already starting with Bill. Going numb from the closeness of him. Thinking it wasn't love I'd felt because I stopped feeling the easy pleasure. I'd never stayed long enough to know what happened after that.

59. IN A NEW COUNTRY

PASSENGERS CAME DOWN THE aisle, passed us in our two-seat row, window for me, aisle for Bill. They put bags in overheads, *click click* of seat belts. The flight attendants walked behind them, *snap snap*, shut the doors of full overheads. Bill put his arm around me. He put his head next to mine and whispered. "This next part is going to be even more romantic than Mexico City." He ran his hand up my leg and pulled me even closer.

I patted his hand. These seats were too small and too close, and it was hot.

We'd had three nights and two days in Mexico City and now were on our way to Oaxaca and after that to Puerto Escondido for the rest of this two-week vacation. This was my first big trip. On a plane! To another country! Bill had planned it all, booked it all, read up on hotels and restaurants. In the month before the trip, he kept telling me how much I would love it, how special it would be, how romantic. Him and me! Two weeks alone together! I packed plenty of books and magazines and looked forward to the quiet time, away from work and home and no one asking anything of me.

An older woman came down the aisle. She smiled at Bill and me cuddled up together, like she loved seeing all this love. I was too warm. Sweat damped behind my knees and spine and trickled down between my breasts. "Wow," I said. "It's really hot." I shifted, and he had to let go.

We'd been together over a year, and I'd moved in with him a few months earlier. We were still mostly everything-is-green happy. But the green was darkening, not so fresh, not so tender. Bill expected honesty and would call out deception even when the deceiver was blind to it. He knew I had trouble being honest about what I wanted and didn't want and hoped he would guess right. He knew how quickly my easy way could turn to anger, and my anger was raised voice, fierce and sharp. I knew he could be distant for days when he felt hurt. I missed our easy, falling-in-love days. Now our love had cuts and scrapes, dark spots and browned edges.

He put his arms around me again and pulled me even closer. "Twelve whole days." His breath was warm and damp against my ear. "Just you and me." His arms so much around me that he could have lifted me out of my seat and onto his lap. His love was like too much sugar, too much sweet. It filled me over-full and I found it hard to breathe. I didn't want him to know, because this trip had been perfect so far.

Perfect, perfect. But I'd never been with someone who wanted so much of me. At home I had my work, me gone for nine hours, five days a week. He had his work, him gone for twenty-four hours every third day. We had our friends, separate and together; we had our families. We'd never been together like this. All-day-every-day us.

And now we were flying off to a new place and twelve more days alone together.

"The market is supposed to be really big," Bill said. "We can buy stuff for all the kids. Plus it's known for their black pottery. And rugs. We can get some for the house." He already loved my nieces and nephew and I already loved his. Now he was inviting me to make his house my own.

"I can't wait to see the hotel," Bill said. "I think you're really going to like it." He moved his hand up my thigh. "I think you're really going to like what I'm going to do to you when we get there." His mouth on my neck and a small twisty knot in my stomach.

My smile felt like a stick-on smile. "Yes," I said. Relevant to nothing. That twisty knot a little bigger, a little twistier.

Bill sat back. Tilted his head, like for a better view of me. "What's going on?" He took his hand off my thigh. "Aren't you having a good time?"

"I am." It sounded flat and false. How could I not be? I had a passport! I had a bikini! I was traveling with the man I loved, and he loved me back. Why did I want to unsnap this seatbelt and run down the aisle and out the door?

I tried again. "I'm really having fun." With an exclamation to it. "Really. Really. Fun." I squeezed his hand. "And I love you. So much."

"Good," he said.

I smiled the smile again and patted his arm. He looked at me a moment longer. He smiled his own stick-on smile and patted my thigh. He moved his hand away and picked up a magazine from the seat pocket.

The last trickle of people came down the aisle. A woman with long wavy hair, a man with a beard. Another man.

This man.

Tall. Slim. White untucked shirt, loose khaki pants. Sandy hair, strong nose, blue eyes.

Blue eyes quick on me. Mine quick on him. Quick like maybe it didn't happen. Then again, like it did. A breath-catch in my throat. He went by.

I waited one long breath, two, three. Sat up straight, raised my arms in a stretch and turned and looked over the seat back. That man was about ten rows back, putting his backpack in the overhead. He chatted with the woman and man who were with him. He looked my way over the woman's shoulder.

His eyes, blue. My eyes. Open.

I didn't blink. He didn't turn away.

His friend tapped him on the shoulder and he did turn away. I sank back in my seat. Closed my eyes. Another long breath.

"You okay?" Bill said.

"Yeah. Maybe a little kink in my neck." I pretend-stretched again. The man had taken his seat. I couldn't see him.

The plane taxied. The flight attendant gave the seatbelt-works-this-way, exits-are-there-here-and-there and in-case-of-an-emergency directions.

Bill put his arm around me. He rubbed my neck. The plane moved fast, faster, fastest. "I can't believe how happy I am to be here with you," he said.

He was too bare, too easy, too much. I didn't hug him back or smile or let my body relax in his arms. That man might somehow be able to see ten seats ahead to this man loving me and I wanted him to know, maybe I wasn't so interested in this man loving me.

I pulled back, shrugged off Bill's arm. "Can you not?" It came out tight. Mean and foul in my throat.

Bill's cheek had that small tremble. "What is going on with you?" His eyes hoped for me to say something kind, something loving. Here it was again: *how easily I could hurt him*. A flash so brief it was gone before I saw it.

"No," I said. "Nothing is. I'm sorry. I don't. I'm maybe nervous to fly." The lie came out with an edge of defiance. What was happening? Why had I taken this turn?

"Maybe I'll read. It'll take my mind off it." Off what? This love right next to me so big I felt swallowed by it? That stranger ten rows back drawing all my attention like a magnet, pulling me even if I didn't want to go?

Bill's eyes were on me as I reached for my bag, found my book. I rubbed his hand like that would make it all better. I opened my book.

Bill put his head back on the headrest and closed his eyes. He was the distant one now. His one long sigh called to the better part of me. The part that knew this was my old way, my hurting, hiding way. The part that answered: Don't do this to him. You were going to be the woman who didn't hurt him. Don't. The page of the book felt rough under my thumb.

We were in the air. We were free to move about the cabin. I put my hand on Bill's leg. I moved toward him; I kissed him. "I'm sorry," I whispered.

He opened his eyes. "Why?"

I couldn't tell him it was because his love was too much. That would hurt him too much. "I. For. I know I sounded cranky. I'm sorry."

"Okay," he said. He eyes went glassy. He rested his head again on the headrest. His jaw clenched and unclenched. I knew this look. This was his gone-away look.

I moved fast from regretful and ashamed to mean and distant and angry. Inside me: *If he couldn't see I was sorry, then fine. If he couldn't see I needed space, then fine.* His distance was a dark relief.

I stood up, careful, stretched my legs over Bill and into the aisle. Down the aisle. That man was there, his head was down.

Look. Look at me. At. Me.

He raised his head. We held eyes, one row closer, two rows closer, right next to him. Past him. I went into the toilet and took my time in the cramped space. Squirt of soap, rinse under the tiny faucet. I slipped the lock open and folded back the door. He was there, waiting in line behind two women.

Eyes on eyes. I blinked. I moved past him. The space was so tight, my arm against his arm. Almost like it didn't happen. I was sure he watched me all the way back up the aisle. I looked. He looked again.

No. No. Don't. Don't do this.

I nudged Bill's shoulder with my hand. He moved his legs so I could get past him to my seat. I picked up my book. Felt the secret in me. That man back there, this one next to me. I put my hand on Bill's thigh and squeezed once, twice. He kept his hands to himself.

When we landed, Bill only said what had to be said as we got off the plane and collected our bags. He had taken a step back. Closed his love away. I missed it like I missed the too-hot sun when I came inside to a cool room.

The taxi driver took us through the outskirts of Oaxaca, dust and sun, board and aluminum houses. Closer to the old city center, there were more people. Men on the streets in jeans and sandals; women in skirts and dresses, their long black hair loose and in ponytails and braids. Bill sat by one door and I sat by the other. Even the driver didn't try to talk.

Our hotel was right on the zócalo, and the zócalo was crowded with people. The driver dropped us off. We carried our bags toward the hotel. On the zócalo, music played with drumbeats and flutes. Inside, the hotel lobby was cool. Water flowed on tile in a fountain in the courtyard, and purple bougainvillea bloomed in pots.

Our hotel room had blue tile and red-and-yellow woven blankets and a window that looked out on the zócalo. Cinnamon and chili scent floated up from the restaurant below along with shouts from the street. A vase on a stand next to the bed held flowers. Maybe Bill had planned this too. I didn't ask. His shoulders were more curled in than usual, face shut down. He stretched out on the bed. I lay down next to him and touched his hand.

Drumbeats out the window, chanting voices.

"Are you okay?" I said.

He was still and silent. I felt bad. He was punishing me. I'd been a little bit mean, a little bit quiet, a little bit attracted to another man. And he didn't even know that part.

The drumbeat, the chanting was closer. I got up and went to the window. A parade of people moved along the street. They were all dressed in white, shorter and darker-skinned than the people we'd seen walking the business area in Mexico City. They carried signs, and they chanted.

"There's some kind of protest," I said.

Bill said nothing.

I wanted him to come back to me. "Let's go see." My voice was pretend-nothing-is-wrong. The sidewalks and zócalo were filling with people. There were men in uniforms.

"I'm tired, Jackie," Bill said. "I'm going to take a nap."

"C'mon." I sat next to him on the edge of the bed. The chanting was louder.

"I don't know what's going on with you, but something is," he said. "You've been different ever since we got on the plane." He held his eyes on my eyes long enough that I looked away.

I took a breath, ready to tell him he was wrong.

"Go for a walk," he said. "Think about it. I'm tired." He closed his eyes and folded his hands on his chest.

"Fine." I took my purse and went out the heavy wood door. At the top of the stairs, I turned and looked at the closed door. I didn't know what to do when he went away like this. When it was me that sent him away like this. I went down the stairs and looked back up, like leaving breadcrumbs, part hoping he'd come after me. I'd never been in a strange city all by myself.

The people in white marched like a parade in the street around the zócalo. Arms up and down with signs printed in red and black paint on white poster, words in a country where I didn't speak the language.

I was alone in this city and this was a protest, and maybe I shouldn't be out here. Maybe I should go back to the room, to Bill and his pushed-away love shoved down deep.

Maybe I would keep walking around.

The man from the plane stood at the curb. He was alone, no sign of the man and woman he had been with. How could it be, just like that?

I went to the curb and stood almost close to him. I looked the other direction, like I didn't see him. The protesters came around again, chanting, drumming. My chest held the heat and the rhythm of the voices and this man next to me. Him alone, me alone. I pretended I didn't know he was there until I looked left, where he was. A surprise. "Oh," I said. "Hi."

He smiled down at me. That strong nose. His pale skin. "You were on the plane."

"I was," I said. "You were too."

The drumbeat in me. A familiar rhythm.

"Do you know what this is about?"

"It's something about an election that's happening," he said.

"You've been here before?" We were talking, like two tourists. But underneath, my stomach thrilled with this new old familiar.

"Not in Oaxaca," he said. "But Mexico. All over. You?"

I was a completely new woman to this dangerously safe unknown man. "No," I said. "My first time." Like I was alone. Like I was that kind of woman. Like maybe he hadn't seen the man next to me on the plane, touching and holding and loving me.

The crowd pressed behind us and we were jostled closer. "Sorry," I said, and he caught my elbow and looked into my eyes. His eyes went down to my chest, back to my face. Where would we go? What would we do? And then what?

And then what?

The thrill turned swirly and sick. This old saying came to me: You can take the girl out of the country, but you can't take the country out of the girl. Here I was. New country. Same girl. I was sick of myself.

I glanced back at the hotel, the dark window of what was maybe our room. The man who loved me was there, hurting. Sweat slid down my spine, made my thighs tacky.

That dark window called to me as though Bill was calling to me. *Come back. Tell me.*

No one had asked so much of me before. To love. To be loved.

My scalp burned. The skin of my hand, the strap of my purse, it all burned. I was fearful not of this stranger but of what it would mean if I turned away from him. If I stepped back. The sun was burning his pale skin already.

"I have to go," I said. It sounded as abrupt and rushed as it felt. "My boyfriend is waiting for me."

"Oh, okay," the man said. He turned back to the street and watched the protesters move along as though I'd never been there at all.

Back through the crowd with the drumbeat behind me. I

entered the cool of the lobby, not missing the sun at all. Up the wide tile stairs, the metal latch, the heavy door. Bill still rested on the bed. He turned to me. His eyes were open, glassy and distant.

I went to him. The drumbeats and cinnamon and the scent of flowers held in the air. I sat on the edge of the bed. Bill shifted over, just a little.

I said, "I want to tell you something."

60. I DO, NO MATTER WHAT

Our wedding was another April wedding, ten years and a few weeks after my first. Spring. My favorite season. Everything is green.

I wore another simple dress but carried a real flower bouquet this time. The flowers on the cake were real flowers and not made by Mom, because Mom only did cakes for first weddings. And, anyway, I hadn't asked her.

We invited my family and Bill's family and good friends.

We wrote our own written vows.

We married in a Chinese restaurant.

Years later, Mom would say to me, "You were so beautiful when you married Bill. You glowed." I felt glowy inside. This was the wedding I wanted. These were the people I wanted to share it with. This was the man I wanted to be with, travel with, explore with. The man I wanted to know and be known by, to fight with and make it through the fights with.

I'd gone on that double-date, blind-date, Chinese dinner date with Bill three years earlier. It had taken so much to get here. I would stay. No matter what.

The day before our wedding, a long white box of flowers arrived from Hawaii. Birds of paradise, anthuriums, red ginger. They were from Bonnie, my old friend who had been so sure about not having children that she'd made it permanent with surgery. I hadn't seen her since she moved to Hawaii. Her note said she was thinking of us, she was happy for us.

Even far away in Hawaii, Bonnie was the one woman I thought of as my touchstone for a childfree life. The flowers were like a sign from her: *this way, all clear ahead.*

Bill and I greeted our guests as they arrived. The nieces and nephews clustered around us: JD, Eric and Jared, Annilee and Shannon, Christy and Kim. They loved the one each of us was marrying as much as they loved their own aunt, their own uncle. In a picture, the young ones around us lean in. Who can be closest to the groom, the bride?

Susan witnessed our marriage. I had no idea how soon I would be calling on her for help with my childless question. Amy witnessed too. She hadn't married or had children, but she would soon. I didn't yet know how our choices would break Amy and me apart.

I held my newest niece Alyson for the first time. In the photograph of this moment, the women at the wedding circle around. They touch Alyson's head, amazed by her thick dark hair. I remember how they asked Cris questions and cooed and ohhed and spoke the language of women to new babies.

Each of the women in the photograph already had a child or would go on to have a child. All of them but me.

61. A PATH TO SOMEWHERE NEW

Plans for a life can change in one moment. A rainy road, a van coming toward a small car at the wrong place and the wrong time. A man with a knife who decides you are the one. Change comes even when you try, so hard, not to be changed.

A few weeks after Amber died, a friend invited Bill and me to a Christmas party. Sparkling white-light tree, wine, small talk with people I didn't know. Eventually, our hostess made her way to us. "How are Amber's parents doing?" she asked.

The glass of wine I'd had rose to a tightness in my face. "It's really hard for them," I said. "Nothing can make it better."

We'd been with Jeff and Patti through phone calls and funeral home, choosing an urn and sorting pictures and picking music. The funeral. Patti saying, "What do I do now? How do I go on without her?"

Her new life without her child.

My friend put her hand on my forearm. "And you?" she said. "How are you doing?" Her hand was warm, and I wanted to feel its comfort.

I wished I had the right answer. There was nothing simple in it. Amber was gone. Her parents had to face this loss, and

Bill and I wanted to help however we could. It would be a marathon, not a dash.

In the face of their loss, I felt ashamed that the tears caught in my throat weren't only for Amber or her parents. A hollow place had been left in me when the child-wanting had finally gone. Like an old habit, I kept reaching for the longing. But it wasn't there.

A memory had come back to me on the night of Amber's accident while we waited in that small waiting room. A memory over twenty years old. The caregivers had come in one at a time, each delivering more news. A nurse, doctor, a social worker. The social worker spoke in a low voice, and her movements were slow, like we could all be startled away by anything too loud, too sudden. She offered what might be offered. Coffee, blankets, directions to the cafeteria, instructions for dialing out on the phone, help finding answers to questions we might have.

Watching her, I remembered something I'd lost. A loss big enough that I'd buried it. Before the rape, I'd applied for an internship for the last step of my schooling. I wanted to be a medical social worker. I wanted to be a calm presence for people during terrible times. When I got an interview for an internship at the local hospital in Eugene, I thought I was on the way to my future.

But, three days before the interview, I was on an examining table in the hospital, covered by a thin blue gown. A detective, and a forensics technician stood nearby while a doctor searched for hairs and fibers and semen and fingerprints on my body.

On the following Tuesday, I'd gone back to the hospital. My plan to keep going forward, to not be changed by the rapist, meant I would keep the appointment. I would have the interview; I would get the internship.

The head social worker invited me into her office. She gestured for me to sit in the guest chair in front of the desk and she took her seat behind the desk. She opened a folder and looked at a paper. I figured the paper was something the internship coordinator had sent over about me. The woman asked how I was.

"Fine," I said.

"I understand you were in here on Saturday morning." She leaned toward me. The light came through the blinds behind her, silhouetted her body. "Your name came up on our report for people to follow up with. I thought I could do that while you're here."

I kept my face completely still and tried to hide the heat underneath.

This was another kind of ambush.

I was here for a job.

"I'm okay," I said, showing her my strength.

"It's a horrible thing that you went through."

Whatever words I might've had about what I wanted to do for work, or how I felt about a man taking my safety, or about this woman prying into me, jammed up in my chest. I sat there, as quiet as I'd been that morning of the rape. My careful plans taken.

She didn't tell me about the job, or ask what I wanted from the internship or my goals once I finished college. She told me about resources and asked if I had anyone to talk to. She gave me a list of counselors. Told me what I might expect in these days so soon after being raped.

She didn't offer me the job or call me later to offer it. I must have felt disappointed. Angry. The unfairness of it. But whatever I felt got shoved down with all the other feelings I was working so hard to quiet after the rape. Even this memory got shoved down, until the bitter rush of it came on and mixed with the grief of what had happened to Amber.

I'd needed an internship to finish my degree. Time was running out. I took a placement working with drunk drivers. A job that led to years of work in chemical dependency treatment, which I found fulfilling. That job led me to my current career in human resources. But it wasn't what I'd planned. And, because I needed to not be changed by the rape, I forgot to remember what I had planned.

I didn't want to be a medical social worker anymore. That was a memory, an unfair cost of being raped. And the human resources work I was doing constricted me now, like a once-pretty dress shrunk two sizes too small.

For years I'd been distracted by baby wanting. The dream child had fed an imagined possibility for some other kind of happiness. I didn't want a baby anymore.

Bill listened while I cried, while I talked about this new feeling in me. This unnamed longing.

"Are you tired of this?" I said. "Do you remember when I was happy? When everything was easy with me?"

"I remember," he said. His eyes did look tired. "You're going through something now. Stay with it, see what it's about."

What I loved about him. The ways he encouraged me to know myself.

"I wish I could quit work," I said. "I want some time to figure out what to do next."

"Jackie," he said. "We've talked about this."

We had. Once, twice, twenty times over the past year. Me wanting to quit, him wanting me not to. The money, the plans he had for retirement, which included me working until at least fifty. That meant I'd need to stay another eight years in a job that paid too well for me to look for another.

He said, "You keep wanting things, new jobs, going back to school, like it's something out there that will make you happy. I'm worried you'll quit and still be unhappy. I don't think this is about the job."

What I hated about him. The all-knowing that I couldn't seem to speak against.

A FRIEND SAID, "I look at your beautiful garden, your house, even the way you dress. It seems like something is trying to rise up in you."

The walls in our home were painted in warm colors and hung with art and photographs of all the people we loved. The shelves were decorated with vases and figures from our travels, arranged to tell a story.

Every spring, our garden presented a new canvas to shape. I'd learned what plants preferred to be where, how to amend the soil, what colors and textures drew the eye.

Maybe my friend was onto something.

She said, "Maybe you could explore the creative part of you that drives all that."

I'd never thought of myself as creative.

"There's this book," she said, "*The Artist's Way.*"

Another self-help book. But I was still a searcher. And I was desperate.

I bought the book and dove in.

The primary task in that book was to write daily pages. Like the good student I'd always been, having an assignment pushed me. Each day I started with a word and no intention about where it would go. Another word followed. Words that led to sentences about being a child, about being a girl and then a woman. I wrote about love and sadness, joy and resentment, and the day-in-day-out job that no longer fit me.

As can happen with writing with no intent other than to be open, unfinished business showed up on the pages. What happened to me when I was twenty and a man broke into my life and raped me came to me again.

The fear and anger and sadness I'd pushed down all those years ago rose up. Took my breath. Stunned me. What I had gone through. Some days, as I wrote, I cried. Some days I stopped writing because it was too much to remember. Some days the pages went on and on.

Even though I hadn't wanted the rape to change me, it had. I began to make the connections. One thing had led to another, and I was changed without ever knowing it was happening. My cleaning and control of my body, the way I startled more than others, the pushing away of compassion, nightmares of intruders, the continual awareness of death, the stepping away from pleasure that sometimes happened when Bill and I made love.

Here, with the distance of time and the safety of the life I'd created, the writing released what had been held.

One sentence became a hundred, then a thousand. Pages became notebooks of pages that took me on a path to somewhere new.

Looking up after hours of writing, time gone by, I felt the ache of sitting too long, of being lost in work that took all of me. I didn't know what I was doing, and the writing wasn't yet good. But this felt like something I would do forever.

62. THE BALANCE OF THINGS

LATE ON A RAINY afternoon in the spring of 2002, I drove us north on I-5. Bill and I had just finished a weekend class in Eugene, and the excitement about what we'd learned was like another passenger joining in on the conversation.

As the windshield wipers beat back and forth, we talked about one of the concepts the teacher had presented. The need for reciprocity in relationships. A balance of giving and taking. If one person gives too much and the other doesn't find a way to give back, resentment enters.

In some ways this seemed obvious. But sometimes the giver doesn't know they have given. Or the taker doesn't know they've been given to. Sometimes we are blind to the most obvious things.

Pretty soon, the sky turned to dusk. Our conversation ran itself out. Anyway, I needed to focus on the road.

Bill rested his head on the headrest. He closed his eyes. I wished it wasn't raining so hard and slowing us down. I wanted to get home and unpack and have a quiet evening before the workweek started.

Thoughts about what needed to be done at work tomorrow crowded out my excitement from the class. The sinking Sunday-night-weekend's-over feeling made its way into the car and bumped aside the passenger of new learning.

I felt trapped. The thought of going to that job—day in and day out, for who knew how many more years—put a dread in my belly.

"God, I hate to think of going to work tomorrow." I glanced sideways eyes at Bill. Hoping he'd agree I should hate it. Hoping he'd see what was behind my words.

He kept his eyes closed. But he was awake. I could tell by the press of his mouth, the small tremble in his cheek. His silence fed the gray, the dread. It nudged aside the closeness I'd felt for him all weekend.

He could at least agree, at least nod, at least open his eyes.

I'd started a writing project about the rape. I planned to find other women the rapist had assaulted. To see how they had come through it after all these years, and what was the same or different from my own coming through. I'd already interviewed one of the detectives on the case. His story of the police trying to catch the rapist had opened a whole new way of seeing how the impact of rape ripples out beyond just one victim.

The more I wrote, the more I wanted to write. I wanted to spend more time in the small room off our bedroom. That room no longer held the exercise equipment it had been filled with the day Bill's aunts whispered that it could be a nursery. Now the room held a desk, a chair, a computer.

"I wish I could quit," I said. A little louder, a familiar pleading sound in my voice. "I'm sick of it."

The windshield wipers went back and forth, back and forth. Bill didn't move. My words were old news. Not-even-worth-listening-to news.

I knew what he was thinking. *We had such a good weekend. Why can't you just enjoy the moment? Why do you have to spoil it with this same old complaint?*

Water fanned up from trucks. The wiper blades weren't doing much good. I wanted to shout at him. *Listen to me. Look at me. Say something. Can't you see how hard I've worked to please you? To not burden you with my wanting.*

I wished he'd say, *You should quit your job. Write full-time. I love you. I want you to be happy.* To say it wildly and enthusiastically. Like I used to wish he'd be about having a baby. *You want one, so I want one too.* Whole conversations I'd had all to myself and then went on as if I'd had them with Bill.

His eyes were open now, as though he heard my thoughts through the harsh cut of water against metal. He stared straight ahead at the window, the rain, the road. His shoulders drooped down. He looked worn out.

He was sick of my wanting, my needing, my changing plans and agreements. I was sick of him not seeing what I'd given up for him. For not swooping in to save me.

Traffic had slowed for the rain. I eased up on the gas and made space from the car in front of me. I looked back and forth from the road to Bill. His profile. The curve of his head. His now mostly gray curls.

I opened and closed my hands on the wheel.

"I gave up having a baby for you." My voice was easy, direct, calm. This surprised me. It seemed so simple to say.

"I wanted a baby," I said. "But I wanted to be with you more." The rain still came, the traffic still moved, the wipers still beat. "I feel like you owe me for that."

Bill turned his head toward me. He was listening. This wasn't about him. It was about me.

I looked straight ahead, through all the gray.

"I don't regret it," I said. "I'm even glad." The desire for a child had gone. But the resentment had held. "But I struggled for a long time. I hurt from it. That you didn't want a baby with me. That you wouldn't do it for me." My throat felt tight and open all at the same time. "And I didn't want to make you wrong for it because I was the one who wanted to change the plans."

He turned completely toward me. "Wow," he said. "I didn't

know." His voice had a bright and genuine lift of surprise. "I didn't know how hard it was for you."

I wanted to slam the brakes, to jerk the wheel. To yell at him, *How could you not know?* He'd seen me holding all those babies, my love for them plain as could be.

I couldn't stop myself from saying it out loud. "How could you not know?" My sharp knife of accusation, *You should have known.*

He pulled back. The tremble in his cheek, I knew it from all the years. Him vulnerable. Me too. I didn't want to push him away. I didn't want to stop what I had started.

"Wait," I said. "Don't go away." The rain and the traffic forced me to calm my breath. I wanted to understand. I needed to understand.

I softened my voice. "I'm just—I'm surprised. That you didn't know."

"I knew right after we got married," he said. "That conversation with your mom. But after that, I thought you were mostly okay with it. You said you were okay with it."

It was true. I'd tamped the wanting down. Held it constricted and bound inside me. Hidden from him. Hidden from the world. Only sometimes letting it out in hints and wishes and wonderings.

I had told him I would be fine. I'd said, "Don't worry."

That was my way. Learned when I was a child, and these were the rules of family: *Hope someone reads your mind, guesses right at what you never say you want. Don't demand. Don't take. Don't ask. If you do, it will hurt worse when you don't get it.*

And Bill, who had no hiding filters, had believed me. Believed my silences and trusted I would not hide.

"I would have done it," Bill said. "Remember, I told you that if you really wanted to, you could have a baby."

Yes, he had said that. More a surrender to my wanting than something he wanted.

"You did say that," I said. "I remember."

I remembered the *you*. *You could have a baby.* Not us.

Prisms of white headlights moved in one direction and red

taillights in another. What I had wanted and he had wanted. It was complicated. One of us giving up was the only way.

If I had taken Bill's yes and run with it, the scales would have tipped in the other direction. He would have had the power of having sacrificed his own wants. It was easier to be the one who gave up what she wanted than to risk being the source of his resentment.

Bill put his hand on my arm, moved it up to my shoulder. He seemed so open, so trusting.

He had bent and shifted too. I was the one who had changed the rules. His side of the scale could be weighted by the number of times he'd said yes, willingly and enthusiastically, when I said, "I want this (A new house! A degree! A class!)." But he was never measuring.

Now he didn't bring up his own giving, or the burden he had to have felt in my wanting a child.

He simply said, "I'm sorry. I didn't know how hard it was for you. That you did it for me."

I put my hand on his leg and he reached for it. The air in the car felt lighter. Just the two of us here.

Maybe it wasn't him I'd given up a child for. Maybe it was for me. Leading to this moment, held in the power of love and other possibilities. It was me I owed. To stand up and declare my plans. To not wait for someone else's approval.

"I'm going to quit my job," Not an ultimatum. Not a question. Only my open heart, my sure voice. "I'm going to write full-time."

What I had missed all those years ago was that when I was certain and acted on it, Bill became sure too, and he fell in love with my enthusiasm and what grew from it.

"Good," he said, "Do it." His voice held same clarity as mine.

And, because I was a woman who had worked all those years, a woman who didn't have children, and he was a man who plans carefully, a man who didn't have children, we had enough saved. I could take this time to write, to shed what was and discover what was next.

He would have loved our child. He already loved my writing.

This was the balance of things.

The balancing was easy. Of course it was easy. It took years for this one moment to be easy.

"All right," I said. And I drove us the rest of the way home.

63. THAT LOVE WAS A MEMORY TOO

Balancing begets balancing. For many years, most of my friends were women with children. I got the vicarious taste of mothering through them. But now, unbidden and unplanned, my friendships grew to include women who didn't have children. Most of these women were sure, had always been sure, and they called themselves childless by choice or childfree. Or they didn't use *child* at all to define themselves.

Other women called themselves childless by circumstance. Sometimes the circumstance was poor timing: no man in their lives and being of a generation that discouraged women having children on their own, or because their love was for a woman and their fertility had happened during a time when it was forbidden or, at a minimum, more complicated, for two women to have a child. Or, like me, they were with someone who didn't want children.

Others had faced infertility. Some of these women were open about their regret; some found wisdom from acceptance of what is.

What should I call myself? Childless by circumstance, from being with a man who didn't want children? Or by choice, because I chose him and never chose children? I decided it didn't matter as long as I defined myself by what I had, rather than what I didn't have.

I was like a woman who'd been thirsty for so long and she finally found water in the place she hadn't been looking. A surprised relief filled me daily. Relief at no longer carrying the weight of resentment. Relief that the wanting was gone, and in its absence, joy was a frequent presence. The relief was most intense when I talked with women friends who were still wishing for a child.

The English friends, Jan and Alan, whose marriage we'd witnessed in Greece, had been trying for a child since not long after they married, and the story of that trying was present every time we visited them in London.

They tried the regular way, then fertility treatments, then adoption. Disappointments and delays became a part of their lives. They kept us updated on the progress, which sometimes didn't seem like progress at all.

On one of our visits to London, after they'd started the adoption process, Jan and Alan showed us how they'd added on to their home to be ready for a possible little girl from China. Another bedroom and bathroom, a larger kitchen, a secret garden with a place to play in the trees and green.

They showed us how they'd made one of the three bedrooms into a child's room. I admired the room politely. For Jan, this expansion was for just one thing: a home ready for her future child. But I was happiest that the addition to their house meant a guest room when we came to stay. And our own bathroom.

In the mornings, I went into the almost-empty bedroom meant for the little girl they hoped for. Jan kept the hair dryer there for us to share. I looked in the full-length mirror at the room behind me as I dried my hair. Pale green walls with pink border, white shelves holding dark-haired dolls. A few stuffed animals on the floor.

I felt a flash of sadness, and couldn't tell if it was in me, or in this room. Jan had held her longing for so long, kept her heart around this possible child.

The sadness shifted away quickly and left behind a calm sense of relief. My old ache for a child was a memory in me. Like someone I'd once loved, now long gone, and that love was a memory too.

64. THIS MOMENT

DAD'S DEATH IN 2004 came fast and burned us all, like a rope slipping through our hands. Only three months passed from the time his skin began to turn yellow to the time of his death, four days short of his seventy-first birthday.

The minister came out to the ranch to help plan his funeral. When she finished, she asked us to stand together in a circle in the family room. Mom, us kids, spouses, and grandkids. The minister prompted us to say whatever thoughts we had about Dad.

Someone said what a good storyteller Dad had been and how he knew the stories of the ranch and the people in town, those who were alive and those who were dead. A visit to the cemetery with Dad was like a history lesson of the whole county.

Someone said how good it was with Dad, these last twenty years with him sober.

I said I liked watching him with the grandkids. That even though I didn't have any grandkids for him, he sure loved those he had.

Mom, in her grief or her thoughtlessness or whatever it was, said, "He was always disappointed that you didn't have kids. He didn't understand it."

Her words were the knife I'd cut myself with for the past fourteen years. Again, I'd invited this in and it tore into my grief. I wanted to yell at her for saying this now. For saying it ever. For even thinking it.

I said nothing. This moment wasn't about me.

The minister asked us all to bow our heads and join hands for a prayer. I was glad to bow my head. I took hands with the nephews on either side of me, tried to rein in the hurt and anger. The minister started the prayer, and I started crying. Tears for Dad not being here to stop Mom from saying I'd disappointed him. He'd never held it against me. I liked to believe he accepted his disappointment as his own.

Mom saying he wasn't fine with my choice really meant she wasn't fine with it. Maybe she never would be. No matter how old I got, or how happy I was without children, the ache for her approval would always be with me.

65. FAULTS CRACKED OPEN

OVER THE NEXT YEARS, that long-ago learning prodded me again: death comes quickly and suddenly. Chances to clean up unfinished business can be lost.

Old friends came to mind. I picked over memories, thought of the people I'd let go. Two friends especially: one who had children and one who didn't.

BONNIE WAS MY FRIEND who'd announced over a lunch of salad and tiny pink shrimp that she was going to have a tubal ligation, that she didn't want children. Then she made that choice permanent.

She'd moved to Hawaii. This was long before email and social media made staying in touch easy, and our contact had dwindled after she moved. One of the last times I'd heard from her was when she sent that bouquet of flowers to our wedding.

Even though Bonnie and I didn't talk, all these years I'd thought of her as the friend who had done what I'd done. She hadn't had children. She'd been sure, certain, final. My touchstone.

I'd never tried to contact her. Maybe I hadn't wanted the full validation of a life lived without children. Not until now. Now I wanted to know how her childfree life had turned out.

I dug out an address book and dialed the last number I had for her, the one from Hawaii. For sure it would be a wrong number.

She answered on the fourth ring.

"Bonnie?" My voice held my surprise.

"Yes?" she said, like a question.

"It's Jackie. Jackie Shannon," I said.

"Oh wow!" It was as though we'd talked just last week. "Jackie," she said. "It's so good to hear your voice."

She sounded so familiar, and yet the years gone by made her voice new to me.

We did the back and forth of catching up.

And then came her news.

"Well, I guess there is one big thing that's happened since I saw you," she said.

A marriage, I thought.

"I have a girl. A daughter. She's eleven."

A daughter. Bonnie had a daughter. She'd switched plans on me. I felt a moment of betrayal. She wasn't supposed to switch plans. This thought embarrassed me. As if I had any more right to talk her out of having a child than I'd had to talk her into it all those years ago.

She'd married a man who wanted a baby, and she'd had the tubal ligation reversed. She'd changed her plans for this man. More than eleven years ago.

"It didn't save the marriage, but we made this beautiful girl," Bonnie said. "She's the best thing I've ever done."

I said all the things. How surprised I was. How cool. That I was happy for her. I always thought she'd be a good mom.

"Hang on a second," she said. "Are you near your computer? What's your email?"

A few seconds later, a picture. Bonnie's blond-haired girl leaning forward over the back of a horse jumping two cross rails.

I poked around inside myself, trying to find the old sore spots. All these years I'd held Bonnie in my mind, told myself if she could be fine without a child, so could I. But she'd made a child happen. She had this beautiful horse-riding girl.

I was surprised it didn't hurt. What I'd said was true. I was happy for her. Happy her girl was in the world.

Bonnie asked about Bill. I told her we were still together. Still happy.

"I always knew you two had a good thing," she said.

"Yes," I said. "We do."

Her girl's hair was brilliant blond, the color of Bonnie's. She loved horses like Bonnie loved horses. She was strong.

It took me longer to turn back toward Amy, my once-best friend from Eugene. By the time the prodding of death pushed me, seventeen years had gone by. Seventeen years while the child she'd had in her belly during that long-ago earthquake grew into a man.

I'd told myself it was normal, a friendship can run its course, things changed, we went different ways. I believed this with a belief so strong that it grew brittle, and any thoughts of Amy felt dangerous. Believed this until enough time had passed. Until being childless was solid and firm in me.

I put her name in Search and found her on Facebook. A dangerous thing, to send a light email. To friend an old friend you had abandoned.

"How are you?" my message said. "I've been thinking of you."

It was messy and thoughtless. I wanted to be back in contact and wanted to skim over the possible hurt my turning away had done to her.

Her fierce response came a few hours later. Wild, and full of her anger. "You are offering to be my friend after seventeen years? You are not my friend."

Then more messages came, one after another, full of the pain of those seventeen years.

I read, answered stupidly, defensively, justifying with small reasons why I'd cut off contact.

Her messages back: "It hurt." "That doesn't make sense." "I was your friend."

Over the course of days, we kept at it, long enough for me to begin to question my reasons for turning away from her. Long enough that small faults cracked open my own story. What I couldn't let myself see back then: It had been too hard to watch Amy have what she had. This one specific friend. Having a child at exactly the time when my body, my dreams, my womb, craved this, too.

I used to not believe in regret. I saw it as a denial of our own actions, actions based on doing the best we could with the knowledge we had at the time. How can you regret a decision if you didn't have all the information, even if the information is hidden under a cloak of self-preservation?

But I had to look clearly at what I had done to Amy. I'd hurt her. I couldn't pretend I hadn't.

With the persistence of old friendship found again, Amy and I found our way back to each other. To a place different than we would have known had I been present for the raising of her son and the son that came after him. The loss of those seventeen years is a scar that holds absence and the thick healing that comes with truth and forgiveness.

66. THIS PARTICULAR HAPPINESS

MY PLAN TO FIND the other women who'd survived the rapist led me not to them, but back to myself. With the distance of twenty years, and the safety of the life I'd created, writing carved trails to my memories. I began to accept what I'd fought so hard against. The rape had changed me; it had wounded me. My tidy ways, my tidy body, my ever-vigilant ears and eyes and easy startle, my need for control—these were the surface scars.

Healing would not come from finding the others, but with myself. Even so, sharing and writing about what had happened to me led other women to tell me their stories of assault. *So many other women.* In this way, I was not alone.

My love for writing expanded. I was a beginner and didn't know what I was doing. I started taking classes. Alongside essays I wrote about the rape, short stories came out of me like they'd been stopped up inside forever, waiting for me to invite them out. Stories about liars, stories about the unspoken words between parents and kids and husbands and wives, about cats jealous of babies, and how a conflict can start over the simple matter of which way a car is parked.

The classes introduced me to a whole community of writers who helped me shape the stories and find the courage to send them out in the hopes of publication.

ONE EVENING AT HOME, Bill was upstairs watching the news and I was downstairs in front of the computer, checking messages. I clicked on one. My whooping shout of happy and my call—"Bill, come here"—brought him quick.

Later he would say he knew exactly what had happened the moment he heard my shout.

"I got a story accepted." My smile had taken over my whole face. "In a journal. I'm going to be published."

Bill stood beside me at the computer and we both looked at the message from the editor. A person I didn't even know had read my story. He wanted to publish it. Bill took my hand. He pulled me up to him and wrapped his arms around me. "I'm so happy for you."

We stood there in our celebration embrace, present in this particular happiness. Even though the publication was my victory, it also felt like something we'd done together, all that had led us to each other, all the work since, that Sunday drive home, our reciprocal balancing.

I called Mom right after. Over the years she'd become a different kind of reader. Like mine, her tastes had moved away from romance books and Sidney Sheldon novels. We shared most-loved books back and forth and talked about them on our Sunday afternoon phone calls. I respected her opinion.

A few years earlier, Mom had asked to read the manuscript I'd written about the rape. I went to Condon for a visit one weekend and gave it to her. She started reading immediately and read late into the night for two nights in a row. When I came downstairs the morning after she finished it, she had a look that I couldn't remember ever seeing from her.

Her face was bright and the light of her was full on me. She said, "Jackie, you're a beautiful writer." She said it was hard, reading what had happened to me then and in the years after. She said she was glad I'd shared it with her. She hoped I'd keep writing.

Since then, she'd asked to read everything I wrote.

Now I told her my news. "That's so wonderful." The excitement in her voice, the way it lilted up, felt like returning to a special place with her, a place only she and I could share.

Long ago, one late night when I was three, or four, or maybe five, I couldn't sleep. I left my bed and went down the dark stairs and into the family room. Mom was there in the lamplight, reading or drawing, TV down low. I told her I couldn't sleep. She could have been upset, me coming down and interrupting her time. The quiet was hers in those late hours when all us kids were in bed. But she reached for me and had me stretch out on my side on the sofa. She put my head in her lap.

She must have said something, told me to close my eyes, told me that everything was going to be okay. She lifted my pajama top and caressed my back, her warm hand against my skin. I had her all to myself, and she had me all to herself. This was the mothering. This was the daughtering.

67. TEMPORARY ALLOGRAFT

IF YOU PUT ANOTHER'S heart or lung or kidney in your body, your body will fight it. You must take drugs to lower your immune response, so your body can accept the foreign tissue. A zygote (an embryo, a fetus) carries the unfamiliar genes of the father as well as the familiar of the mother. The zygote has its own genetic code. It is a foreign body.

The mother's body must persuade itself to let down the fight, to not attack the strange thing. This zygote is considered a temporary allograft. It must stay within for those months, the mother must carry it, host it.

Sometimes the body does reject, or the temporary allograft resists, and the future baby is lost. But most times, her body takes care of the child. It turns its own immune response on low flame. She must avoid risks. No raw fish, no raw eggs, no sushi, no deli meat, no soft cheeses. And so on.

A mother practices these cautions to bring her child safely into the world.

And then she tries, we all try, to keep this child safe.

ON A BLUE SPRING afternoon in 2007, after a visit to the dentist, I stopped to water my vegetable garden before going into the house. Pea shoots, bent up from the soil; small leaves of lettuce and beets and carrots in rows. I love spring and all the possibility that comes with it.

Bill came out of the house and said to come inside. The absence of his smile, the stillness of his face; I turned off the water and put down the hose.

He waited until I was in the kitchen, standing by the island. He said, "I have something to tell you." And he told me.

Cris's second girl, Devin, had taken her life. She was fifteen.

My knees didn't buckle and I didn't cry out, but you can fall apart in a hundred ways. A silence took over, shut my ears. I wished the silence had taken over earlier, before Bill had said what he'd said.

Her mother. My little sister. Being so damn careful through her pregnancy, falling in mother-love for Devin when she arrived, guiding her through the toddler years, almost losing her once when she was struck by a slow-moving car; worrying over her problems with reading and focus. Cris did everything she could think of to help Devin, even when Devin broke the rules, even when Devin was angry with Cris for doing what a mother must do to shepherd her child to adulthood.

The story of Devin's death is another story, not mine. The story of my sister's pain, the pain of her family, our family, of the town. We couldn't understand what had happened.

But Devin remains with me. I am still her aunt, she is still my niece. Death cannot stop this. Thoughts of her will come in on seeing a horse or a cow or a long-haired girl with a perfectly curved forehead, a border collie, a basketball, rhinestones and grommets, a country song, a gun. On hearing the line of Shakespeare that, as a little girl, Devin broke and made her own: "To be or not to be, is that a question?"

When Devin was seven and Alyson eight, they came from Condon for a weekend visit. That first night, Bill was at work. Alyson fell asleep on the couch, but Devin asked to sleep in my bed. Maybe she was a little nervous being away from home.

We tucked in and I turned toward her. We talked for a while. It was getting late, so I pretend-closed my eyes and slowed my breath, thinking that might help her settle. She thought I was asleep.

Eventually, she turned onto her back and I opened my eyes a little and watched her. She soothed herself by laddering her thumbs and fingers like Itsy Bitsy Spider and whispered, "You have the power. You have the power."

I thought I might cry at the hopefulness of her. What power did she need? What magical giver was she whispering to? I brushed the hair back from her head and immediately regretted it because she stopped.

A YEAR OR TWO before Devin died, the family had gathered for Christmas Eve. Mom, us five kids, our spouses. The nieces and nephews. Tawna's girl T'Lee, the first great-grandchild, born the year before Dad died.

We had dinner. The tree. All of us getting ready to open presents. Someone hushing someone else, someone saying, "Hurry up, we're going to do it now." One of the kids, said, "Aunt Jackie, we have something for you. It's from all of us." JD and Tawna, Annilee and Shannon, Alyson and Devin and Joely were standing together. One of them handed me a gift bag.

Inside, under the red tissue, was a small pillow. It had hearts and embroidery. Not like what I kept in my house. "Oh," I said.

"Turn it over," one of the kids said.

On the other side, in dark lettering: *AUNT: A cherished friend and personal cheerleader who will always see you through 'rose' colored glasses.*

I'd loved them all of their lives. Helplessly. Fiercely. To be revealed in this moment was almost an embarrassment. My first impulse was to make a joke of my love. But I stopped myself. I said, "Thank you." And I let the tears be.

When I chose not to have children, I made a bargain with the child-giving, child-taking powers. A bargain I hadn't even known I'd made until Devin died.

Yes, I'd agreed. *I will not have children. My task will be to find*

peace with this. The love I would have given to my own unmade
children will be an added protection for those who are here.

This was the agreement.

I would see when they were struggling, and reach out. My hands were free.

I thought my bargain would keep them all safe.

But it did not.

Being childless wouldn't protect them. It wouldn't protect me. Even so, it won't keep me from the stunning pleasure of witnessing a child in her pure moments, or of loving her even when she is gone.

V.
THE JOY I'VE HAD ALL ALONG

68. MOST OF THE TIME, THIS IS ENOUGH

I'M WELL INTO MY fifties now. Between Bill's side and mine, I am aunt to over thirty nieces and nephews, and great-nieces and great-nephews. I held many of these kids just days after they were born, some on the day of their birth. With those who are married I count their husbands or wives as my own, too, and the children of friends. So that number is even bigger.

The young ones call and ask for play dates. They rush to the door with wide arms on arrival and ask to please stay longer when it's time to leave. The older ones turn to us for advice: where to go to school, how to interview for a job, how to breathe through a panic attack. They deliver their big news personally: a good report, a winning game, an award, an engagement, a new job, a baby on the way.

Most of the time, this is enough. But lately, there's been a surge in baby news. Annilee and her husband are waiting for the call to come get the boy they're adopting from Colombia, their first child. JD and his wife are trying for their second child. Last Tuesday, Shannon called to tell us she's pregnant with her first.

Leanne will be a grandmother soon. Will it hurt? Will this be a whole other kind of loss? Will the edge of regret cut?

Women who are grandmothers say, "It's the best. You have no idea." I don't think they mean it literally. They forget that I truly have no idea what it's like to be a grandmother, and I never will. They're caught up in their own joy. I try to stay caught up in mine.

They say, "I get all the fun of having the grandkids and none of the drudgery." This part I know. It's the joy I've had all along.

Leanne's girls turn to her for preparing advice. They'll turn to her for mothering advice. She's the one who's been through it.

She buys baby gifts for her soon-to-be grandchildren and helps paint and set up the babies' rooms. I help some of the time. I buy gifts too. But I'm careful my gifts aren't too many, my offers to help aren't filled with my own needs.

Our grandmother, Nana, didn't like the ways Aunt Lena competed for our attention. Nana got priority; she owned the grandmother territory. A grandmother gets less time with her grandkids than she did with her own kids. She doesn't need a break like a mother might need. With grandchildren there is less time to share.

Wanting something deeply leaves traces, grooves for regret to grab hold of, even when the wanting is gone.

I'm not yet bitter or lonely. But I keep lookout on myself. The nurturing mothering in me holds. I turn my focus outward to all that I have and with an eye to where I can give without stepping on the territory of others.

69. TINY TADPOLES OF LIFE

IN 2011, WE VISIT Alan and Jan again in London, and they give us an update on the adoption. It could be months. Or it could be years. It could be never. Alan is turning forty soon. Jan somewhere past that. Their wanting holds strong.

"So we're trying something else. A surrogate."

A donation. Sperm. Tiny tadpoles of life.

"First one didn't take," Alan says. "But it's possible we'll be calling you with news in a few weeks."

The night before we leave London, we celebrate their anniversary and talk of their beautiful sunset wedding in Greece. We have dinner and wine and champagne. Bill and I make moves to go up and finish our packing.

Jan says, "There's one last thing we want to do." She and Alan take us to their backyard. It's a lush and varied and smells of roses and green. Ever since I first saw it, I've pictured children running in all that grass, picking the flowers, scaring the wood pigeon that parades in the mornings like he owns the place.

"We have these Chinese lanterns." Jan holds out two plastic-wrapped squares of white paper. "We light them and let them go into the sky. You're supposed to make a wish."

"Well, we all know what we're going to wish for," I say. I am a little drunk, and a lot happy.

The white lanterns are tissue paper and wire. One for Bill and me, and one for Jan and Alan. They unfold theirs first. Jan holds it while Alan touches the lighter to the wick. It won't go to flame. Then it lights low and goes out. Then the flame from the lighter burns the tissue. "Oh, no." Jan's voice breaks, like all her loss and waiting has come down to this: a lantern with a wish that won't fly.

Bill nudges me with his elbow. "Hold this." I take our lantern from him. He takes theirs, drops it on the flagstone, and kneels down. He begins to tear at Jan and Alan's lantern.

"What are you doing?" I say, worried that he's ruining the moment.

He doesn't answer. He keeps tearing until he holds the fuel packet in his hand. "Hold up the lantern." He points at ours. "You and Jan," he says. "Hold it up." The paper is thin, and I hold it with the end of my fingers. Bill puts the fuel packet from their torn up lantern onto the fuel packet of ours. "Light it," he says to Alan. Bill reaches for another corner of the lantern, so it expands. I trust him, and feel drawn to his confidence.

We're all quiet, holding our corners, looking down to where Alan holds the flame. The flame takes. It comes up fast and strong. The lantern glows yellow. It pulls and lifts. "Let it go," Jan says.

We stand, heads tilted back. The white light goes up and up and up, over the roof, holding there for a moment, then past the roof, up and out, higher and smaller, but still bright.

JAN AND ALAN DELIVER the news to us on Skype. Their faces are fuzzy on the screen. Bill and I are side by side, our faces tiny in the corner of the screen. "Twins," Alan says.

Bill is smiling. "I'm excited," he says and his voice lifts in a way that I recognize. He is excited.

Two heartbeats. Double lantern flame.

"We'll have our hands full," Alan says. "We'll want you in their lives."

To see them have what they've wanted for so long.

"We'll be there." I'm being pulled into something new, all these miles away, across all the land and water, and I can't turn from the pulling.

70. A CURE FOR HIVES

NOT LONG BEFORE HE died, Dad told me about the drive through Fulton Canyon. He said it was a pretty route and meant less time on the freeway. He always took it when he and Mom made a trip to The Dalles or Portland. Ever since he told me, whenever I go to Condon, I take Fulton Canyon too.

Mom is with me today. She had a doctor appointment in The Dalles, and I'm driving her back to Condon and staying for the weekend for Shannon's baby shower. The women of Condon will celebrate as another of their hometown girls becomes a mother, as Leanne becomes a grandmother.

Fulton Canyon has plenty of curves going up a steep grade that tops out in wheat fields, fallow one year, planted the next. This year they're planted. We pass two pretty farmhouses with leafed-out trees, and a bare-wood windowless church.

Mom's eyes are on the puff-clouds against the blue sky. "I've always liked looking at the clouds," she says. "Ever since I was a girl."

"Me too," I say.

She no longer lives on the ranch. Now she lives in an apartment in town. This is the first time in her life she's lived alone. She says she likes it even though she misses Dad, especially at night when she wakes and thinks he's there next to her.

It's harvest time, but the field we're passing hasn't been cut yet. It's a good crop, with thick stalks and full heads. A slight breeze moves the bearded wheat. Slow waves of dark gold shift to pale gold and back to dark gold.

I raise a finger off the steering wheel and point in the direction of the field. "Pretty."

Mom looks. "I guess." Her voice has a halting, not-agreeing sound.

"I've always loved it like this," I say. "Right before harvest."

She shakes her head. "I know it's supposed to be pretty. But I get anxious every time I see a field of wheat waiting to be cut." She keeps looking at the field and hunches her shoulders up and down. "Anything can happen. Fire. Hail."

For sure she's thinking of the hailstorm that came through Condon in '75. It was her birthday. That storm caused a flood down Main Street, knocked holes in so many roofs that a roofing crew spent months in town repairing them. Our whole crop was wiped out. Insurance took care of the loss, but it was awful seeing all the wheat knocked down a month before harvest.

Exactly twenty years later, again on Mom's birthday, another storm came through and caused almost as much damage. This time tennis ball sized hailstones came in sideways and knocked holes in the siding of houses.

"I feel way better when it's all cut," she says. "Even if I don't have to worry about our crops now." The land is leased out, it's someone else's concern, and Mom gets paid no matter what. But she spent fifty years as a rancher's wife. The worry of it is an old familiar trail in her.

"There you go," I say now, and raise my finger again as we pass a field of stubble. Cut-off stalks bent this way and that, no oceany waves or heads of bearded wheat. It looks broken and worn.

Mom turns to look as we pass. "Maybe people think that's ugly." The tracks of trucks and combine have laid bare the fine, dry soil. "But I like it."

We get to the end of Fulton Canyon and go through Wasco and on to Highway 206. We're quiet for a while. She rests her eyes.

"Hey," I say, when she's opened her eyes and resumed watching the landscape. "I've been wondering something."

She's gotten used to my wondering, and I've gotten over being surprised by the open way she responds now.

When I was writing about the rape, I'd asked her if I could interview her. She said yes immediately, no hesitation, even though we hadn't spoken of the rape since it had happened more than twenty years earlier.

We'd sat together in the kitchen for that conversation. I asked her how it was for her all those years ago, when I called and told her I'd been raped.

She looked at me and her eyes got teary. She said, "I watched over you." She said she hadn't wanted to bring it up because it might hurt me to talk about it. She worried about my weight loss back then, and how much I exercised. Worried maybe the rapist had HIV and maybe I did too.

Then she pointed to the kitchen sink. "I started keeping the knives under the sink." Because that was the one thing she knew about what happened to me, that he'd used a knife from my kitchen. She thought putting the knives away might help me not be reminded.

She'd been watching over me all these years. Her unspoken gestures of love.

My understanding of Mom shifted then. Like so many years before when we'd argued about the older man I was living with.

All I want is for you to be happy.

My shifting moved her too, like plates of land lifting and settling into a new landscape. Since that talk in the kitchen, we are more open, less guarded. Mom knows I want to talk about the personal things and she seems to want to join me. As much as she can bear. She's a more private woman than I am. We meet each other here, between my wants and her limits.

Now, as we drive up the grade after the John Day River, I ask Mom, "How did you not get pregnant all those years between me and Cris?"

She'd had the first four of us in less than five years. Then eight went by before Cris came along. I thought of the tiny yellow pills that were my morning ritual for so many years. Did they even have them back then? Or maybe they did but they weren't easy for a small-town woman to get a prescription for.

"For a long time, I used spermicide," Mom says. "This was before the pill. I'd go to Espy. Remember him? The pharmacist?"

I do. I remember his son, too, sandy haired and dark-eyed. Cute. One of the nice boys who was just a friend.

"When I'd ask Espy for the spermicide, he'd say, 'Do you want a spermicide boy, or a spermicide girl?'" She smiles a remembering smile. "I guess he didn't think it worked too well. But it worked for me." She raises her hands like she's as surprised as Espy was.

She laughs. "He was always saying funny things. One time I was getting the spermicide and he said, "You and Jack are the kind of people who should have fifteen kids. Your kids are all so good." She's proud of what she and Dad made.

WOMEN HAVE BABIES FOR plenty of reasons. Because it's the order of things, because they want to make life with the person they love, or because they aren't careful. Maybe they want to be loved or want something to love. Maybe a woman believes a child will bring happiness. Or that she has something to give or teach or learn. Her body longs for that temporary allograft. She can't imagine life without a child.

"Why did you want children?" I ask Mom.

We pass the mountain identifier, and I glance to see the Three Sisters, Three Fingered Jack off in the distance.

"It's what we did. I didn't think about it, really. It's what women did then."

She says, "I wanted a boy and a girl, so I had Pat and then Brad, and I kept trying after Brad. And I had Leanne." She's told me before that she loved being pregnant. That it was easy, the pregnancy, the labor.

She says she might've stopped after Leanne. "But I got a terrible case of hives, not long after she was born. It was awful. One day a spot on my leg would be red and swollen. It burned and itched and hurt. Another day it would be my neck or my arm or my back. A lot of times it was my mouth." She touches her mouth when she says this part, her hand remembering the pain. Her mouth, like mine, thin lips, small even teeth. "I went almost a year hoping they would go away. Then I asked the doctor if he thought it would help if I got pregnant. I'd heard that somewhere.

"I'd have done anything," she says. "Being pregnant was way easier than those hives." She hovers her hand over her mouth and then her thigh, like the hot red pain is still there. "The doctor thought maybe it would help." She smiles. Her voice has an uplift of surprise. "So I had you." Her cheekbones my cheekbones, her thick hair my thick hair. "It worked. I never had them again."

The townscape comes into view at the rise of the last hill. We're about a mile from Condon. The trees and houses, the grain elevator with the Christmas star turned off this time of year.

These conversations are our way now. Mom gives me her stories, and I give her mine. If I'd had children they would have been our bridge. Without them, we found this other way.

"I've had some ups and downs," I say. "With not having kids. It was really hard sometimes."

She looks to the south. We both look to the south. The ranch there. The house empty now. Five kids and none of us taking over the ranching life. Our silence holds the missing for Dad, the years of our family on that place.

"Watching Leanne become a grandmother," I say, "I guess not having grandkids is a whole other thing I'll be having feelings about."

She doesn't say, *I told you so.*

We're at the edge of town. The wide streets, tall trees, a boy running a lawn mower.

Her silence makes me bold. "I've worried that what you said might come true. That I'd end up being a bitter, lonely old woman."

"Did I say that?" she asks. She sounds surprised.

Words that had been crashing around inside me all these years, she doesn't remember.

"Yeah," I say.

The knives others throw down, and we pick up and use as weapons on ourselves.

"That wasn't very nice of me," she says.

I could be angry that I took in her words, carried them in me. It was so long ago.

I pull up in front of her house, the gravel gives under the wheels.

What she said back then took me someplace I wouldn't have gone, helped me keep watch on myself, made me determined to have another kind of life.

"You won't be lonely," she says. "Look at all the kids in your life. You wouldn't have had the time for them if you'd had your own. And all the friends you have."

The garden in the big house kitty-corner from Mom's apartment is full of summer bloom, gold rudbeckia, some tall purple flowers. Asters maybe.

"And you aren't bitter," Mom says. "You've got Bill. You're living a happy life."

71. BABYLAND

IT'S LONDON-COLD AND WINDY when we come out of Gatwick Airport and find our way to the pickup area. I'm pretty sure this is the place where Alan said Jan would meet us.

Their babies are ten weeks old.

We've come from Switzerland, where it was sunny and we witnessed the marriage of Raphael, the son of our Swiss friends, and stood with the parents for pictures.

Now in London, the wind picks up and blows a sideways mist at us. Bill keeps looking at me and I keep looking at him. We speak a whole conversation, shaped by our years together, translated with raised eyebrows and tight smiles:

Where the hell are they?

Fuck it's cold.

Are you sure this is the place they said they'd meet us?

Why didn't you make the arrangements if you don't trust me?

Do something.

I check my notes about the pickup plans. None of the cars lined up by the curb have Jan in them.

Bill says, "Maybe we should call."

"Let's wait." I'm an expert on this. All the years with my friends, my sisters, me waiting by the door with the diaper bag, while the mom talks the kid into shoes they don't want to wear or out of too-hot galoshes they do want to wear; or me holding the baby while the mom grabs one more blanket, one more toy, one more something just in case.

Bill's eyes are on me again, question eyebrows.

Babies. Babies make you late.

WE ALREADY MET THE babies, Dylan and Poppy, on Skype, just a few days after their birth. Alan called us from the pale green room that had been empty the last time we visited London.

Poppy was awake, her new baby eyes unfocused and dark. Dylan was asleep in his crib. Jan and Alan had just brought Dylan home from the hospital because he'd needed extra care. He was underweight and having trouble keeping food down.

Alan turned the camera to himself and Jan. They both had dark circles under their eyes. "The babies aren't sleeping well," Alan said. "A lot of whingeing."

Back when they were waiting for the babies to be born, Jan and Alan said we should come to see them in the first few months after. I thought that might be too soon. Shouldn't it be the new grandmother coming to stay? But Alan's mother had died many years ago. Jan's mother would help with these babies, but she had other demands she couldn't turn away from.

"Really think about it," I'd said. "Make sure it's the right time for us to come."

On the Skype call, when the babies were here for real, I checked in again. "Are you sure you want us to come now?"

"Yes," they said. "We need help, whenever you can come."

After we hung up Bill said, "I can't wait to meet them." He had a smile and his voice had a lift to it.

I'd never seen him like that, excited about babies.

"Jan and Alan are exhausted," I said.

I'd only ever been with new babies for a few hours. I'd never been asked to come stay. I'd never been asked to help.

•

Now I turn in one direction and Bill turns in the other direction, hoping to see their car.

Finally he calls out behind me, "Jackie, look." Jan is next to him, smiling.

"Hey!" I say. "You're here." I go in for a hug. I stop. That's no purse in her hand. It's a baby carrier. A baby in that baby carrier. "Oh! You brought—"

"Poppy," Jan says. "This is Poppy."

Round ball of a head, red tint to the barely-there hair.

"She's beautiful," I say.

"Isn't she?" Jan's eyes are soft with tired, and something else. Love, I guess. "Alan's with Dylan, getting him ready for the next feed." She looks at her watch. "Which we need to get home for, before this one wakes up, screaming for hers."

All the way from the airport, we talk about schedules and feeds and them not coming together to the airport because of schedules and feeds and baby seats and a car not big enough for all of us. We talk about Dylan's problems with keeping formula down. Poppy begins to cry and then to scream. I'm next to her in the back seat and I try to soothe her, which only works for a moment.

Here we are. Babyland.

The dining table has been pushed against the wall and is now a place for baby carriers, diaper bag, diapers, wipes, changes of clothes. Dylan is in his carrier. I have Poppy in her carrier and I set her next to him. Bill and I stand side by side in front of Dylan. He's awake. He holds one fisted hand near his chin.

Alan is behind us, hands on our shoulders. "It's really good to have you here."

"They're beautiful," I say. The thing you say.

Poppy is beautiful. The flush of her skin. But Dylan. "He's so tiny," I say.

Dylan's unfocused, dark blue eyes move toward the sound of us. Beneath smooth baby skin, his pallor is gray. His forehead is creased, three lines across, two tiny lines between his eyes. Where Poppy is full cheeks and round belly, Dylan is angles and wrinkles, dark hair and worried frown. They'd told us he was underweight, but seeing him, I feel scared for him.

Bill leans in over Dylan and speaks in a low voice, "Hi Dylan. Yeah. There's the boy. Hey, there. Hey buddy." Bill is so present with this baby. His voice is gentle. Maybe he feels scared for Dylan, too. I think he's glad to be here meeting these babies. I'm used to him being playful and interested in kids. But this is new to me, to see him so interested in such new babies.

ALAN TELLS US HOW they've started Dylan on a medicine and a new way of feeding him that should help him keep a high-calorie formula down.

I step closer. Dylan's eyebrows are small arches like worry. This new world is light and noise, and the pain in his stomach.

Poppy wakes, fists and arms, her face goes to pink, to red. Her mouth opens into a tiny circle. She cries.

"Sorry, guys." Alan moves to her. We step aside. "They'll be whingeing and we won't get ahead of it if we don't do it now."

Time to change them. Time to feed them.

My stomach growls. Usually, when we arrive, we have a glass of champagne right off. Dinner would be ready. Now the kitchen is filled with washed bottles and nipples, formula and bibs, dark bottles of dropper medicine.

I sit on the bar stool next to Bill. We watch Alan and Jan feed the babies they've waited so long for, like we're watching a movie. Bill reaches over and takes my hand. He looks at me like he's checking to see how this is for me. Maybe this is a look of worry. Maybe it's a look like, *Ta-da! Here are some babies for you.*

Alan feeds Dylan and explains the process. Twenty milliliters, then take the bottle from his hungry mouth, lean him forward with his knees bent up to help him release trapped air.

This is a special way of burping. Or winding, as Alan calls it. I imagine gusts of air, trees bent, not a tiny bubble trapped in a baby's belly. Alan rubs his hand in circles on Dylan's small back. "Don't pat. He has to wind at least once before he can have more. He hates this first part because he wants to eat." To prove it, Dylan begins to cry. "You can imagine," Alan says. "He must be so hungry."

I can imagine. My own empty own stomach makes noise again.

Feed and wind. Feed and wind. For an hour.

Finally, Alan mentions champagne. Dinner.

Thank god.

Alan looks at me. "Will you hold Dylan while I start things?"

I move to the sofa and Alan passes him to me. "You'll have to hold him up," Alan says. "He has to stay upright to keep the formula down." This is a different way to hold a tiny baby. I want to show Jan and Alan that this is natural for me. I want them to know I can help.

I cup Dylan's tiny foot in the palm of my hand. Baby toes. I put my little finger in his hand. His fingers wrap my finger.

Alan pours champagne and hands me a glass. We toast. Jan and I hold our glasses out and away from the babies in our laps.

"To babies." I sip, hold the sparkles in my mouth, swallow. I like champagne. I like holding this baby. I set the glass down.

Bill watches me, and I feel it in a spotlight way. His smile seems almost proud, pleased, like he thinks this is helping me have what I never had. I don't want him to watch me. I want to hold this baby and not think of what might have been.

BILL AND I ARE in bed. My book is propped on my chest; my book-light makes a circled glow on the page. Jan and Alan have finished the late-night feed. I hear them in the pale green bedroom next to us, the murmur of their voices as they settle the babies. Love is in this house.

Bill's breath deepens, lengthens toward sleep.

"What were you thinking when you were watching me hold Dylan?" I say.

There's a long quiet space. I don't know if he heard me, if he's even still awake.

"I was thinking what a good mother you would've been."

Him saying it plain like that. It hurts a little. Here in my belly. A sliver, a shard of my stone of resentment still holding. And in my head, *You have no right to say this now that it's too late.*

"I know," I say. "I would have been."

IN THE NIGHT, I hear a baby cry. Dylan, maybe. Alan's whisper. The lighter whisper of Jan. They talk to their babies. I wonder if I should get up to help. I stay in bed. They are with their babies. This is private.

Later, the house is quiet again. I get up and go to the bathroom. The clouded moon sends thin light through the window. In the mirror, my face looks younger. Smooth skin, hair loose and messy. Like in a picture from ten years ago, twenty years. I didn't know how young I was or that time would pass this quickly.

At our bedroom door, I stop and look to the open door of the babies' room. I try to hear their breath, to see their shapes. The nightlight only reveals the white slats of cribs and the turning shadows of the mobiles hanging above.

POPPY SNUFFLES AT THE bottle when I feed her. Breathe and drink, breathe and drink, like grateful applause. When she's done, I ask Bill, "Ready to hold her?" He's always been good with kids as long as they are at least two years old. Not babies. He never showed an interest. The only infant I ever saw him hold was M'ari on the day I witnessed her birth. Even then, he held her for less than a minute.

But now, right away, he says yes to holding Poppy. He doesn't have to be talked into it.

He settles back on the sofa, and I put her in his arms. I show him how. "Support her neck in the crook of your elbow, or up this way, on your chest."

His shoulders hunch; he moves slowly, that tiniest tremble he gets in his cheek when he's nervous.

Poppy's legs stiffen. "Relax your shoulders," I say. I reach with my free arm. Touch one of his shoulders. He relaxes. She relaxes into him.

Alan puts Dylan in my arms. Little bird legs, soft crown of head.

Bill tilts his head down to Poppy. "Yes," he whispers. "Yeah. That's right. I've got you." He cups the crown of her head. Her eyes go sleepy. Bill looks over at me, and he has the baby-drunk look people get when a child lets go into your arms. The muscles in his face relaxed, the corners of his mouth turned up in a completely unconscious way.

He might fall in love. I might fall in love.

I shift Dylan in my arms, move away from Bill, just a little, to make room for the catch of my breath.

Alan watches us the same way Bill watched me last night. That spotlight shining on a woman with no children holding a child, next to a man with no children holding a child.

The heat of it burns. What we could have had.

THE DAYS GO BY. We hold babies and feed babies and talk about babies and try to help around the house. One day is like the next. It's all babies all the time, and Jan and Alan are lost to it. I begin to feel tired, restless. When we finally go out on the third day, I'm happy to be doing something different.

Going out is a production of stroller and carriers and bags and diapers and finding a space in a restaurant or store big enough for all the stuff of babies. On the street, Bill pushes the stroller. I wish he'd let Alan push the stroller. I wish he'd come take my hand. But he's happy being with the babies.

I walk fast in front of him to look in the window of another store, a blue dress. I can go fast; the stroller can't go fast. I tick off each thing. *I can go into a café for coffee. I can sleep through the night. Go out on a whim to a movie, all alone or with Bill or with a friend. I can read a book whenever I want. Spend the whole morning in my garden. Go to yoga. Write for long, uninterrupted days. I can make loud noisy love and never be too tired.*

UPSTAIRS, IN THE AFTERNOON, I lie down on the bed. Bill says, "You okay?"

"I'm tired," I say. "Really tired."

He puts his hand on my hand. Wraps my fingers. He's worried that I'm so quiet.

"Does being here make you regret it? Not having kids?"

"No," I say. "It's fun, but. I don't know. I miss being home. The babies are so much work. It exhausts me. And it's kind of boring. One-dimensional. I'm glad it's not me." The words are chalky, dry in my mouth.

Had I become the woman Mom worried I'd turn into? Old and bitter? The one people speak of? *She never had children. Didn't want them. Selfish.*

ALAN PUSHES ME TO start feeding Dylan. "Really, it gives us a break," he says.

I hold Dylan's head in my palm, his body along my forearm. It's a long, slow process and, in that long, slow process, I watch Dylan's face. The crease between his eyes is like worry. His eyes stare at me. Feed and wind, feed and wind. There's something about this baby. So hungry. So relieved to have the bottle.

I offer to feed him the next time, and the next.

Bill sits beside me every time. When I pull the bottle from Dylan's mouth and rub the circles on his back, we whisper to him. "That's a big strong boy. You're getting bigger and stronger every minute. Such a healthy boy." I want our words to make it so. He drinks more. Bill cups his hand over the top of Dylan's head. He puts his thumb lightly on the crease between Dylan's eyes. Dylan eases and drinks. Bill keeps his arm around my shoulder, his hand on Dylan's head. And we go on that way.

This is what we are here for.

Sometimes Bill sits on the stool and watches me. I still feel the spotlight of his eyes, the heat going deep in me. I let it in.

•

BILL PUSHES THE STROLLER around a big store. I walk beside him. A woman stops us and says, "Oh, congratulations! You're lucky." I grin and feel proud. I point at Jan and Alan. "We are lucky that their parents let us spend so much time with them."

We stop for coffee in the crowded café of the big store. A woman, somewhere past forty with long dark hair and tap-tapping high heels, slows by the stroller. She takes in both babies, looks at Jan. "I wouldn't want to be you," she says with a horrible snort of a laugh. She moves off so quickly I have no time to grab her, jerk her by her long dark hair, take one of those high heels and tap it on her head. Tell her to get some sense, tell her she has no idea what she's talking about, tell her to shut her pie-hole. How fast I've gone from baby-bored to baby-love. Right now, in this moment, I would want to be Jan. I'd take either or both of these babies in a heartbeat. I am too old and it's too late, but I would.

ON THE NIGHT BEFORE we leave, I'm holding Dylan, as I have for so much of the past week. Earlier, when he threw up his formula because I moved him too suddenly, I felt it like a personal loss. "I'm sorry," I whispered in his tiny ear. "I'll do better next time."

Bill and Jan and Alan are talking. Poppy is asleep in Jan's arms. I touch Dylan's forehead, like I've seen Bill do. Maybe Dylan's frown is less worried than it was when we came. His cheeks. I'm sure they are more full.

My chest aches like a hand is pressed so hard it might knock me from this place. The ache moves to my throat, that hand clenching it now. It grows.

Tears come. A surprise and no surprise at all.

Here, I let myself feel everything. What I missed and what I have. Right here, right now.

I look up, let the tears run.

"I've always heard women say that the love for their baby is like nothing they've felt before. I never got to spend this much time with a baby this new. To hold him for hours. For days. To be a part of his survival." I look at Alan, at Jan. "Thank you for sharing them."

Bill comes to sit beside me. He touches Dylan's head, and our hands meet there. "It's going to be hard to leave," he says.

Once the tears have started, they keep coming. Quiet. It's an opening to a place I didn't know I had. As though someone came and found another chamber in my heart. Said, *You didn't have to have a child of your own to know this. It is safe here. Love comes in, just by being open.*

WE'RE BOTH ON OUR backs in bed, looking up into the dark. Our arms touch; our feet touch.

Jan and Alan are in the next room putting Dylan and Poppy in their cribs, saying good night to their children.

Now it is me who asks Bill. "Do you regret it?" I say. "Do you wish we'd had kids?"

Bill shifts so that the full length of our legs touch. "I never understood what you went through before now," he says. His hand covers mine. "Wanting to have children. How hard it was. I didn't realize."

"You didn't see it?" My voice holds the surprise. "How hard it was?"

"I knew what you said," Bill says. "But I couldn't know what it felt like. I never felt anything like that. Never. Not until now."

One of the babies, Poppy, lets out a small cry. Bill stops, and we are both still. Then the room next door is quiet.

Bill says, "I didn't know what it feels like to hold a baby. To just hold them. It's powerful."

Somewhere, sometime long ago, he shut himself off from the possibility. Never opened his arms.

What is worse? To want something and decide not to have it, or to suddenly wake up to the might-have-been that you didn't even know about?

He says, "Being with them. Holding them. To have someone

need you so much. To be able to help him. I'm sorry I kept us from it."

We breathe into the dark. Our hands tighten on each other.

Maybe true understanding comes only from having a loss close enough to another's to recognize it.

Bill didn't keep me from having a child. I chose. I didn't keep myself from anything. My world opened up and I took hold of it.

I say, "I'm not sorry."

It's a beautiful ache, this kind of love.

ABOUT THE AUTHOR

IN ADDITION TO THINKING she would be a mother, Jackie Shannon Hollis once dreamed of being a June Taylor dancer or a race car driver. A lifelong Oregonian, she resides in a home her friends call the tree house. Through her local library, she facilitates writing classes for people experiencing houselessness. Jackie and her husband lead workshops on communication, conflict management, and creating successful and satisfying relationships.

ACKNOWLEDGMENTS

WHEN I BEGAN WRITING, I fell in love with the process, the page in front of me, the way sentences can be shaped to bring forth the experience of a memory. This was a love I expected. What I didn't expect was that I would find a community of writers who support and teach me. What I didn't expect was that my family and other friends would show up with enthusiasm, cheering my successes, and comforting me in my disappointments. I write with the force of this community behind me.

Laura Stanfill took a risk on publishing nonfiction with this book, and I am so proud to be a Forest Avenue Press author. Gently suggesting and asking just the right questions, Laura was a keen guide in the final revisions and on the path to publication. Her fierce spirit as publisher, writer, friend, mom, and human being is a gem of light.

The care of the Forest Avenue Press team helped make this book shine. Having Gigi Little's work on the cover of this book is a gorgeous treat that I get to nibble as often as I want. Maya Myers's careful and loving eye caught all the things, kindly.

Blackstone Publishing gave me the opportunity to tell this story out loud and helped my voice shine on the audiobook.

Rachel Sussman walked with me through many revisions. Her smart eye and belief in my story kept me digging deeper and helped me learn about my own capability as a writer. I am so very grateful to her.

Dawn Raffel's encouragement and editing gave me hope that my story might reach readers some day.

Jennie Shortridge was my early model for how writers can lift each other up, no matter where we are in the process.

My first writing group (Jean Johnson, Misty Haley Bouse, Mary Alice Moore, and Marlene Taevs) welcomed me in and showed me the power of a writing community.

Joanna Rose and Stevan Allred, my teachers at the Pinewood Table, opened up writing for me when, as a new writer, I had the images but couldn't always translate them to the page. Their verbal applause and notes spurred me along and they reined me in when needed.

I've been enriched by the continued conversation with writers I met in those years around the Pinewood Table. Gratitude to Brian M. Biggs, Bruce Barrow, Sarah Cypher, Steve Denniston, Sherri Hoffman, Harold Johnson, Amber Keller, Christi Krug, Mary Milstead, Julia Stoops, and Laura Whittlinger. Liz Prato helps me be bold. Scott Sparling shows me how to be calm in the midst. Mark Lawton reminds me of the importance of connection.

Thursday after Thursday, through writing this book, Cecily Patterson taught me to ride the winds of metaphor, Kate Gray kept me going back again to look carefully, Joanna Rose showed me how to be wondrous about it all, and Yuvi Zalkow made space for my creative and curious heart.

My bond with my family is enduring. They let me tell our stories, even when they may wish I'd keep my yap shut. Pat Shannon, Brad Shannon, Leanne Durfey, and Cris Patnode are the solid posts of my history. Dad taught me how to take my time with a story. Mom taught me to pay attention, and she bravely asked to read everything I wrote.

I have over forty-five nieces and nephews (and grands and in-laws) now, as well as kids of friends who have let me be a stand-in aunt. I held the comfort of many of these children as babies and have known the joy of watching them grow. With them I am goofy and pretend to be wise. With them I feel the vastness of love. A special shout-out to Annilee and Shannon who let me think I have magical powers, and Christy who reaches out each Mother's Day.

Bill's family welcomed me in and helped me know him through their stories. They have expanded my experience of family and love.

My gratitude to those without children who have taken this other path and recognize me when we meet on it. There are so many ways to be in the world and none of them have to be the expected.

The parents who have shared their children with me have also shared the real, true, joyful, and unromantic view of parenting. Berni and Pierre, Jan and Alan, Susan and Bill, Dane and Mary, Pat and Leah, Leanne and Larry, Cris and Joe, Jeff and Patti, Sherry K, Dai Lene, Yuvi and Sheri, Kindel and Dennis, D'nise and Alan, Will and Ajit, Clint and Laura, Sandy, Rene and Gerry, Rena and Dewey, helped me reshape the missing into fullness. And the joy continues as the children have children and they share them too.

Amy Gibson, Bonnie Cordiero, and Stephen Victor taught me the durability of friendship.

Gratitude to my first husband for walking the early path with me.

I am lucky to have been born and raised in the town of Condon. I feel the wide-open sense of home and the embrace of community each time I see its townscape on the horizon.

Michelle Fredette, Dian Greenwood, Kathleen Lane, Kathlene Postma, Gina Loring, and Melea Seward also listened to pieces of this book as it took shape. Thank you to the Oregon Extension for creating a space at Lincoln for us.

If it wasn't for others asking about my progress, I might have given up long ago. Sherry Arisim, Steve Arndt, Russel Baskin, Chris Bernard, Berni and Pierre Blanchard, Jessica Blanchard, Raphael and Carole Blanchard, Will Davie, Leanne

Durfey, Sandy Gunder, Carrie Sue and Cleo Gustafson, Kirk and Sharon Hale, Joanne Hatch, Jared Helbig, Ed Helbig, Annilee Hyre, Mark MacDonald, Gina Loring, Ajit Maan, Jenny McGuire, Jan and Alan Pavett, Donna Rocco, Dick Sass, Jason Sass, Gretchen Sass, and Nancy Townsley keep the pen in my hand. Jane Geesman is my fierce and solid support, and Georgia Cacy and Sarah Lucht make me feel cool and smart.

Jennifer Sass pushed me to begin the first project I ever wrote, which eventually led to this book. If she were here, she would hold this book to heart and we'd both have a good laugh about it all.

Mary Rex helped me understand the layers of myself and taught me that owning my way of being in the world is the biggest part of self-compassion.

Jamie Bosworth made images of me that reflect the inside.

Early readers generously offered careful eyes and thoughtful feedback. I am grateful to Sheri Blue, Joanne Cimbalo, Amy Gibson, Bonnie Cordiero, Jane Geesman, Patti Kaser, Kathlene Postma, Judy Samuelson, Stephen Victor.

Reading another writer's forthcoming book takes a commitment of time and care and reputation. I don't take this lightly. I am honored to have the support of Jody Day, Kate Carroll De Gutes, Leanne Grabel, Kate Gray, Sheila Hamilton, Dianah Hughley, Caroline Leavitt, Kathlene Postma, Liz Prato, Jennie Shortridge, Cheryl Strayed, Yuvi Zalkow, Zoe Zolbrod, and Leni Zumas.

Hedgebrook's generosity of a three-week residency, where the early seeds of this book were planted, sits in a happy space of my memory.

Whole-hearted gratitude to independent booksellers who read and love and sell books, libraries and librarians for creating the safe spaces for books and readers, and to the readers whose hearts the books land in.

A special thanks to the Multnomah County Library and the Writing Through It writers.

My husband, Bill Hollis, always saves the best thing on

his plate for last. He makes me laugh; sometimes at myself, but mostly at him. He encouraged me to tell our story and he read every single draft of this book, each time in one sitting. He helped me understand that secrets burn us and openness expands our hearts. Bill is the yummiest thing on my plate.

THIS PARTICULAR HAPPINESS

READERS' GUIDE

BOOK CLUB QUESTIONS

1. *This Particular Happiness* begins with a quote from *Mrs. Stevens Hears the Mermaids Singing* by May Sarton: "Love opens the doors into everything, as far as I can see, including and perhaps most of all, the door into one's own secret, and often terrible and frightening, real self." How does Jackie Shannon Hollis explore this concept in the memoir? In what ways has loving another opened the doors for you to see your real self?

2. Jackie's mother expresses hopes, dreams, and disappointments for her daughter. How important should our parents' hopes and expectations be? Have you ever felt the disappointment of one of your parents? How did you respond?

3. Throughout *This Particular Happiness*, Jackie questions her motivations for wanting a child. What do you think is a good reason to have children? To not have children?

4. How do you think Jackie's father's drinking impacted her early relationships with boys and men? How do you think Bill's father's distance impacted Bill?

5. Before Jackie's first date with Bill, one friend who knows him says, "He might be kind of boring for you." Another friend says, "I don't know if he's for you. . . I think he likes to party." What do you think she means when she describes this as 'people putting stories on other people'?

6. How do you think Jackie's sexual encounters and failed relationships impact her decision to stay with

Bill despite their difference regarding the desire for children? Why do you think she stays?

7. On a vacation in Mexico, Jackie becomes attracted to another man. Why is this an important scene? How do you think it changed things for Jackie? Have you had a moment in your relationship when you realized the choice you made would change the course of your future?

8. Brief chapters focus on Jackie's husband and his childhood. What purpose do they serve? How did these scenes inform your understanding of why Bill did not want children?

9. Bill remains consistent about his decision to remain childfree. How did you feel about his stance on this, despite Jackie's longing?

10. How do you explain Jackie's sudden urge to have a child? Where do you think the urge to have a child comes from?

11. At the end of chapter thirty-one, Jackie writes, "Knowing where your scars come from doesn't make them go away." In this moment, she is referring to Bill, but how do you think this applies as a larger theme in *This Particular Happiness*?

12. Jackie's experience of her childless decision evolves over time. What does she do to make peace with her decision and to avoid resenting Bill? In your own life, what have you learned to accept, and in turn live with, even though you might have made another choice?

13. How are the tragedies in the book related to the central question of whether or not to become a mother? How have losses in your own life—or in the lives of your friends or family—changed your perspective?

14. What does Jackie learn about friendship? Do you think friendships are as important and complicated as love relationships? What have you learned about yourself through your friendships?

15. Near the end of *This Particular Happiness*, Jackie is driving her mother to their hometown of Condon. They talk about farm life, her mother's pregnancies, and how Jackie came to be, and Jackie reflects on a loving gesture her mother made many years ago. Why is this moment important to this story?

16. By the end of the book we have a sense of a hard-won bond between Jackie and Bill. What strategies do Jackie and Bill use to reach this point in their relationship? What do you think it takes for a couple to find their way through a major conflict?

17. Jackie questions what she should call herself: childless or childfree? By the end of the *This Particular Happiness*, what label do you think best fits? Is there a word that does not include "child" that we could use to describe a woman who has not had children?

18. Has your thinking about people who don't have children changed in any way after reading *This Particular Happiness*? Is there a difference for you in how you see men's choices versus women's choices?

19. In *This Particular Happiness*, Jackie explores family legacy, generational expectation, mother-daughter relationships, alcoholism, sexuality, sexual assault, grief and loss, personal growth, relationships, friendships, sisterhood. What situation in Jackie's life do you most identify with? What surprised you most in this story?

PHOTO GALLERY

Bill and Jackie, 2018. Photo by Jamie Bosworth.

The sign for the Shannon family ranch in Condon, Oregon, where Jackie grew up.

Some of Jackie's ancestors.

Jackie sports a haircut her mother gave her.

Bill and his brother Clint, both firefighters.

Falling in love, circa 1987.

Jackie and Bill on their first trip to Switzerland.

Holding the twins, Dylan and Poppy.

Jackie and Bill and their own particular happiness. Photo by Jamie Bosworth, 2018. Visit jackieshannonhollis.com for an extended photo gallery of people and places that appear in this memoir.

FOREST
AVENUE
PRESS